THROUGH THE EYES OF FAITH

3rd edition
Compiled by
Dr. Jack E. Bower, CPA

THROUGH THE EYES OF FAITH

3rd. edition
Compiled by
Dr. Jack E. Bower, CPA
Eastern University
Associate Professor of Accounting

A Profitable Publishing Publication
All Rights Reserved
Copyright © 2006 by Jack E. Bower

Proudly Published in the USA by
Profitable Publishing
a Division of Thornton Publishing, Inc.
17011 Lincoln Ave. #408
Parker, CO 80134
1-303-794-8888
www.BooksToBelieveIn.com
publisher@profitablepublishing.net

ISBN: 0-9779960-6-9

Preface

SCRIPTURAL ADMONITION TO STUDY ACCOUNTING

Luke 16:1-13

Jesus told his disciples:

"There was a rich man whose manager was accused of wasting his possessions. So he called him in and asked him, what is this I hear about you? Give an account of your management, because you cannot be manager any longer."

The manager said to himself; 'What shall I do now? My master is taking away my job, I'm not strong enough to dig and I'm ashamed to beg. I know what I'll do so that when I lose my job here, people will welcome me into their houses.'

*So he called in each of his master's debtors. He said to the first, 'How much do you owe my master?' 'Eight hundred gallons of olive oil, he replied.' The manager told him, 'Take your bill, sit down **quickly**, and make it four hundred.'*

Then he asked the second, 'And how much do you owe?' 'A thousand bushels of wheat,'he replied. He told him to 'Take your bill and make it eight hundred.'

The master commended the dishonest manager because he had acted shrewdly. For the people of this world are more shrewd in dealing with their own kind than are the people of light."

Jesus makes the observation that shrewd business practices are sometimes not used by believers in God (people of light). Accounts receivable discounting is now standard business practice and terms like 2/10 net 30 are in common use today. Note that the stronger discount included the word "quickly." This passage and the story in Luke 19:23 imply recognition of the time value of money (NPV), but the real substance of this story is in the relationship between the physical and the spiritual world that follows. Continuing with verse 9:

For I tell you, use worldly wealth to gain friends for yourselves, so that when it is gone, you will be welcomed into eternal dwellings.

Who does the manager of accounts receivable represent and who is the master or owner of the estate? I suggest that we are the manager in the story, the stewards of God's creation. The master is God and we are encouraged to give away the physical things that are under our control. We store-up treasure in heaven by being generous with the wealth God has given us to manage, and at the same time we please those who are in debt to God. Humanity is often depicted as being in **debt** to God. This is why Jesus said he was our year of Jubilee (Leviticus 25 & Luke 4:19-21). Through Him our debts are forgiven. More about this topic in chapter two. Now the scriptural admonition to study accounting.

Whoever can be trusted with very little can also be trusted with much, and whoever is dishonest with very little will also be dishonest with much.

What is the little and what is the much? I suggest that the physical world is the little and the spiritual world is the much. Control over the seduction of physical possessions is critical to receiving spiritual property (a man's life does not consist of the abundance of his possessions, Luke 12:13-21).

So if you have not been trustworthy in handling worldly wealth, who will trust you with true riches? And if you have not been trustworthy with someone else's property, who will give you property of your own?

The *Accounting Through the Eyes of Faith* is dedicated to the trustworthy handling of worldly wealth. This passage gives strong admonition to study accounting. The main point of the parable; **Manage the wealth He has given to you, in a trustworthy manner and you can be a manager of God's spiritual property.**

No servant can serve two masters, Either he will hate the one and love the other, or he will be devoted to the one and despise the other. You cannot serve both God and Money.

Yours in Him,
Dr. Jack E. Bower, CPA

PART I

~ Introduction

Chapter 1

THE LIBERAL ARTS AND YOUR VOCATION

THE SEVEN ORIGINAL LIBERAL ARTS HAD A VOCATIONAL FOCUS

By
Jack E. Bower, C.P.A., Ph.D.
Associate Professor of Accounting
&
Frederick J. Boehlke, Jr., Ph.D.
Professor Emeritus of History
Eastern University

One of the more frequently asked questions among college students is, "Why do we have to take courses like 'Justice in a Pluralistic Society' or 'Science, Technology, and Values'? The implication is that the "liberal arts" are a waste of time and that only studies in a "major" like accounting will provide the ability to secure a job. The question deserves a proper response considering the cost of a college education and the fact that the liberal arts or core represents about 46%[1] of the total course work required for a bachelor's degree. The following will help explain what it means to receive a liberal arts education.

The liberal arts were first defined during the early middle Ages in a book titled, <u>Marriage of Mercury and Philology</u> by Martianus Capella. The marriage of these two gods occurred on the Milky Way with the other gods as witnesses. Originally, the seven liberal arts were: Grammar, Rhetoric (effective public speaking), Dialectic (debate) representing the literary arts; Arithmetic, Geometry (including surveying), Astronomy and Music representing the mathematical sciences.[2] It is important to note that these were the "vocational subjects for the clergy."[3] A priest needed the literary skills for sermons, arithmetic to keep the accounting records (accounting was soon to be included in all math textbooks), geometry to settle boundary disputes between farmers, astronomy to set the ecclesiastical calendar and music for worship. **The seven original liberal arts had a vocational focus**.

During the Renaissance, the focus was on a reconciliation of Plato and Aristotle. The effort was actually begun during the Middle Ages by Boethius, a Roman patrician, who held the office of consul under Theodoric the Ostrogoth.[4] There were two domains: the world of Plato, which was a domain of ideas (truth, love, et al.) and the world of Aristotle, which was the domain of the physical and observable (heat, light, et al.). St. Thomas Aquinas, who lived between 1225 and

---

[1] The Eastern University Fixed Core is 24 plus the Breadth Requirements of 34; 24+34/127=.45669
[2] <u>The World of the Middle Ages</u>, by LaMonte, John L., page 81.
[3] Ibid, page 81.
[4] Ibid, page 82.

1275, brought the two worlds together. You may have heard the expression that St. Thomas Aquinas baptized Aristotle.

It was believed that a properly educated person of the Renaissance could operate in both domains. The college student who does well academically and is also skilled in mechanical repairs (fixing a car, for example) as well as playing some musical instrument would be called a "true Renaissance" man or woman. Their broad general education allows them to participate in both the physical world and the world of thoughts and ideas.

The word "liberal" comes from the word liberate or set free. A broad liberal education will set your mind free to dream and create. The word "art" is in contrast to the logic of the scientific method. It should not be confused with the performing arts or the created arts of physical beauty. It is instead a way of thinking creatively about a particular subject. For example, the application of tax law is an art form not a science, even though it would fall into the category of a social science. The line of distinction between the arts and the sciences is often blurred and disputed by academicians. Psychology, for example, can be both a social science and a biological science. Accounting is considered a social science but has its roots in the field of mathematics. The math textbooks of the fifteenth century contained sections on algebra, geometry and proportionality or what we call accounting.[5]

Today a liberal arts education is thought of as a general education including a specialization or what we call a major. Two centuries ago this was not the case. Only the subjects of Philosophy, Latin, English

---

[5] The Development of Double Entry, Nobes, Christopher.

and Mathematics were part of a general education.[6] Actually, the specific courses that constitute a general education have always been and continue to be a disputable topic in educational circles. The evolving debate and the resulting curriculum modifications provide considerable insight into the nature of what we call a liberal arts education. The rest of this article will briefly highlight some of the discussion in a historical context.

Here is an example of the discussion from the Self-Study Committee of Lawrence College as recorded by the Carnegie Series in American Education: The Search of a Common Learning:

"Liberal education **must include** *an exploration, in some depth, of at least one area of knowledge which may be determined by the student's own personal interests* **or by vocational needs.** *Such an exploration, they add, a general education cannot provide; since at best, it can only give an introduction to the broad areas of knowledge from which further exploration must follow."*[7]

The debate of a general education not requiring a specialization to requiring one, progressed slowly over time at colleges around the world.

Medieval education was indoctrination. The goal was to mold the mind into a fixed type.[8] The Renaissance changed all of that and a liberal education was an education of reason and logic intended to dispel superstition and fear. "In the fifteenth and sixteenth centuries the scholars of the Renaissance turned from theological education to human letters."[9] The study of

---

[6] The Search for a Common Learning: General Education, 1800-1960, Thomas, Russell, McGraw-Hill Book Co. Inc. 1962, page 3.

[7] ibid, page 4.

[8] The meaning of a Liberal Education, Martin, Everett Dean. W.W.Norton & Co. Inc. N.Y., 1926, page 32.

[9] ibid, page 33.

the literature of antiquity and languages became the backbone of the liberal arts, what we label the humanities.

By the early eighteen hundreds, a general college education included two courses of study, the classics and the sciences. The core curriculum was defined as: math, language, physical science, biological science, philosophy, religion and history. The longest of the courses of study was in the physical sciences.[10] The social sciences were not included even though their existence was firmly established. The thinking of this time was that the specializations such as law, medicine or divinity should be limited to graduate schools. It is true that graduate schools significantly refine and develop specific areas of knowledge. The problem is that many careers do not require a graduate education so the debate over the inclusion of specializations in a bachelor degree program continued. The debate took a different form at each college. A brief history of the University of Pennsylvania will illustrate the progressive development of the debate.

The great college founders included names like Benjamin Franklin, University of Pennsylvania; John Harvard, Harvard University; and Elihu Yale of Yale University. Some of the founders, such as Benjamin Franklin, wanted a very practical and utilitarian type of education. Franklin's views on education did not prevail however, and it was a source of great bitterness and conflict for him.[11] His proposed curriculum was mathematics, geography, history, logic, and natural and moral philosophy. "It

---

[10] The Search for a Common Learning, Thomas, Russell, page 15.
[11] History of the University of Pennsylvania 1740 - 1940, Cheyney, Edward Potts. U of P press, 1940, page 29.

should be an education for citizenship, and should lead to mercantile and civic success and usefulness."[12] His proposed curriculum was never tested. The trustees of the academy were the most prominent men of the city and the curriculum followed the traditional format of British Schools having a Philosophical School, a Latin School, an English School and a Mathematical School.[13] The next to be added were the History and Writing Schools.

These key liberal arts' courses were considered the "tools of learning." Once learned, the tools could then be applied to various subjects. For example, Latin was a study of structure and expression. All of the subjects focused on the construction of an argument and how to defend it. Educated persons were articulate (Rhetoric) and able to debate a topic (Dialectic). Many scholars of the twentieth century insist we have lost these tools of learning in our general education requirements.[14]

The University of Pennsylvania (U of P) dates its beginnings to the year 1746; the first property was purchased in May of 1740. This date places U of P before either Princeton or Columbia. All of the colleges of this time period suffered financial difficulties from 1791 to 1828. "This was not a great academic age."[15] The colleges that faired the best during these times were the ones with a specific church base or denominational focus. What turned the U of P around was specialization. The Medical School and Law School

[12] History of the University of Pennsylvania 1740 - 1940, Cheyney, Edward Potts. U of P press, 1940, page 29.
[13] Ibid, page 72.
[14] The Lost Tools of Learning, Sayers, Dorothy, Methuen & Co. of London, 1948.
[15] History of the University of Pennsylvania, Cheyney, page 176.

were added in 1791, which increased the enrollment while the liberal arts' departments declined in faculty and students. Other specializations were also added in music, business, dentistry and several other fields. It is interesting to note that history became a neglected subject in the liberal arts during this time period, but was eventually restored.[16]

What does the history of the U of P teach us? The paradigm of a solely liberal arts' education failed. To function in our modern industrial society requires some degree of specialization. In other words, it takes both. A strong general education should include a specialization and together they produce a well-educated person. The dominant accrediting agency for business schools (AACSB) requires that the general education requirement comprises at least 50% of the curriculum. The blending of the two is what makes the American educational system so valued internationally. Various studies, such as Workplace 2000, confirm this conclusion:

"The literate person in the year 2000 will have to be both technically and socially competent. That means that engineers must have an understanding of cultural anthropology and an appreciation of literature, and the English majors need to be skilled with the personal computer and understand science and technology."[17]

A discussion of the significance of the liberal arts should not imply that the specializations are of a lower

---

[16] History of the University of Pennsylvania, Cheyney, page 242.

[17] The Virtual Corporation: Structuring and Revitalizing the Corporation for the 21st Century, Davidow, William & Michael Malone, NY Harper Business, 1992, pages 259 & 260 Taken from Provost's Perspective, by Howard, Harold, Eastern College, 1997.

academic heritage. The study of subjects like music or business principles are as old as the history of mankind yet were not considered a part of the liberal arts' core in the 1800's. The pyramids, a managerial masterpiece, were constructed eleven hundred years before Joseph was sold by his brothers as a slave to the Ishmaelites headed towards Egypt. The oldest known written documents are inventory records recorded on clay tablets. Pope Leo X appointed the first professor of accounting in 1514 at the Sapienza in Rome. This was the highest university of learning in all of Christendom.[18]

Respect for a discipline should come from its lineage and the service that it provides to society. Modern accounting, like classical music, finds its roots in the Renaissance. St. Thomas Aquinas with his refinement of the analogy (Greek="analogos" from which we get our word proportionate) inspired the mathematics discipline of proportionality (double-entry accounting.) Double-entry accounting has been used for over 700 years and has a long history of distinguished professors and scholars teaching mathematics and accounting at various universities all over Europe.[19] Compare this to the development of the natural sciences before the last 200 years. For example, Professor Charles Morton of Harvard (two hundred years ago) was teaching that the annual migration of birds is around the moon, a journey of 200,000 miles in two months flying through space.[20] Many of the specializations like accounting have a heritage or lineage that extends far beyond even the recognition of the liberal arts in the middle Ages.

[18] Accounting Evolution to 1900, Littleton, A.C., U of Alabama Press, 1981, page 3.
[19] Grammateus, a German professor, 1518; Jerome Cardan, 1539, Professor at Pavia and later at Bologna.
[20] Bid, page 5.

Our curriculum will teach you to think critically and to truly appreciate the world around you. We will challenge you intellectually in both the general education courses and in the specialization. Most of all, we hope to strengthen your faith so that you can know and express to others the things you believe about God. Welcome to the world of academia!

Bibliography

Bechel, Paul M. Wheaton College, A Heritage Remembered 1860-1984. Harold Shaw Publishing, Wheaton, Illinois, 1984.

Bell, Daniel. The Reforming of General Education, Columbia U. Press, N.Y., 1966.

Cheyney, Edward Potts. History of the University of Pennsylvania, U. of Penn Press, Philadelphia, PA., 1940.

Dyer, John P. Ivory Towers in the Market Place, Bobbs Merrill Co., N.Y., 1956.

Kenny, Anthony. The Five Ways, St. Thomas Aquinas' Proofs of God's Existence, University of Notre Dame Press, 1969.

Geijsbeck, John B. Ancient Double-Entry Bookkeeping, Scholars Book Co., Houston, TX, 1914.

Howard, Harold C. Provost's Perspective on Higher Education in the 21st Century. Eastern College, PA., 1997.

Journal of Accounting Research, spring 1973, 47-61 & Abacus, December 1973, 137-155 & Nottingham Medieval Studies, Vol. XVI, 1972.

LaMonte, John L. The World of The Middle Ages, Appleton Century-Crofts, N.Y., 1949.

Littleton, A.C. Accounting Evolution, U. of Alabama Press, American Institute Publishing Co., N.Y., 1981.

Martin, Everett Dean. The Meaning of a Liberal Education, WW Norton & Co., N.Y., N.Y., 1926.

Nobes, Christopher. The Development of Double Entry, Garland Publishing, Inc., N.Y., 1984.

Oakley, Francis. Community of Learning, the American College and the Liberal Arts Tradition, Oxford U. Press, N.Y., 1992.

Peragallo, Edward. Origin and Evolution of Double Entry Bookkeeping, A study of Italian Practice from the Fourteenth Century, American Institute Publishing Co., 1939.

Sayers, Dorothy L. The Lost Tools of Learning, Methuen & Co., London, 1948.

Thomas, Russell. The Search for a Common Learning: General Education, 1800-1960, McGraw-Hill Book Co., N.Y., 1962.

Chapter 2

THE FINANCIAL ACCOUNTING ENVIRONMENT

HISTORICAL EVIDENCE THAT YOU CAN'T SERVE TWO MASTERS

by
Jack E. Bower, CPA
Professor of Accounting
Eastern University
&
William Reese, MBA
PriceWaterhouseCoopers
(Senior, Assurance Practice)

The rules for accounting are embodied within a framework of generally accepted accounting principles, commonly referred to as GAAP. The rules for auditing are embodied within a framework of generally accepted auditing standards, commonly referred to as GAAS. Both comprise the essential components of a financial statement audit. Financial statements compiled in accordance with GAAP and audited in accordance with GAAS become trustworthy representations of the financial position, cash flow and operations of a company being audited. It is all about trust. Fifty years ago, the determination and application of both GAAP & GAAS were monitored and enforced by the accounting profession. Now, both are in the hands of quasi-governmental agencies. How and why the transition took place is covered in this brief historical overview. Recent financial history in the U.S. illustrates the impact of greed and provides clear evidence that you cannot serve two masters; you cannot serve both God and money. As a result of greed on a massive scale (recent financial scandals and corporate fraudulent activity), a new era has emerged for the accounting profession.

Society has always needed accountants to maintain the financial backbone of social order. Accounting's sister is the legal profession. Together, they keep the measurement of economic transactions for modern society relatively consistent, comparable and honest. Even in ancient times, accountants were necessary to count the spears, horses or troops. The oldest records known to mankind are accounting records, such as the clay tokens found in Mesopotamia that were used as the first bills of lading.[1] The only time counting was considered evil was the second great sin of King David as recorded in II Samuel 24:2-10. Here are the words of King David:

"Go throughout the tribes of Israel from Dan to Beersheba and enroll the fighting men, so that I may know how many there are."

David was conscience-stricken after he had counted the fighting men, and he said to the Lord. "I have

[1] *"The Roots of Writing,"* Time, August 1, 1977, page 76.

sinned greatly in what I have done. Now, O lord, I beg you, take away the guilt of your servant, I have done a very foolish thing."

King David counted his troops, demonstrating a trust in his mighty army instead of God for his protection. Modern society is also guilty of this same sin. How many people trust their bank accounts and retirement plans instead of God for their security? From God's perspective, it is all about trust. From a financial market perspective, it is all about trust.

THE FIRST BALANCE SHEET

A major revolutionary method for recording and presenting accounting information was created between 1211 and 1296 with the advent of double entry accounting, Dr = Cr and the Balance Sheet, A=L+OE. What caused this algebraic breakthrough in bookkeeping? What created the idea of setting things equal to each other? What was the critical intellectual influence of this time period? The answer is quite obvious; Saint Thomas Aquinas the father of proportionality who lived from about 1225 to 1274 pioneered this new methodology. A journal entry follows his rules of proportionality. (Support for this theory is detailed in chapter four of this book) This new methodology would prove to have a major impact on the accounting environment.

The first to promulgate generally accepted accounting principles (GAAP) was Pacioli.[2] His book was titled <u>Summa de Arithmethica, Geometria,</u>

---

[2] There is considerable dispute over the name Pacioli as it was translated. Some scholars prefer Paciolo. The name used for some of the later books was Fra. Paciolo di Borgo Santo Sepolcro. In certain books his name is Patiolus.

Proportioni et Proportionality, and was first published in 1494, about two hundred years after the earliest record of double entry accounting.[3] It proved an immediate success and was quickly translated into seven different languages. Why was it not printed in 1274, shortly after its creation? It is because moveable type was not invented until the year 1450.

INDUSTRIAL REVOLUTION

The next major event that impacted the accounting environment was the industrial revolution, particularly during the 1920's or the golden age of business. The economy of the U.S. now equaled that of Great Britain, France and Germany combined. The need for accountants was exponential. It was a time of excessive spending and excessive investing by renowned businessmen such as J.P. Morgan, Carnegie, Vanderbilt and Rockefeller. Big business and Republicanism was thought to be good for the country. Unfortunately, much of the financial investment activity was based on fraudulent information. An inverted pyramid was created to scam investors, where new investment money obtained from the sale of company shares was used to pay out dividends generating the illusion of increased profits. During this time, many companies boasted growth only as long as new money kept coming in to cover their lack of profits. The largest of the pyramids was the Koelger & Toll Company. The president, Mr. Koelger was nicknamed

[3] John Geijsbeck, Ancient Double-Entry Bookkeeping, Scholars Book Co. Houston Texas, 1914. The best collections of the works of Paciloli are at the Geijsbeck-Lawrence Library in Denver and at Harvard University Library, Cambridge, Mass. The second printing of the Summa was in 1523.

the "Match King." He committed suicide in 1932 upon discovery. Without the audit function, this type of behavior was inevitable; the dream became a nightmare, ushering in the great depression.

During the industrial revolution there emerged various social dynamics with in the accounting community that changed the accounting profession in profound ways. Public accountants began to refer to themselves as "Independent Expert Accountants." By 1882 there were two groups who competed for representation of the profession, the Institutes of Accounts and the American Association of Public Accounts. The latter organization was primarily composed of former Chartered Accountants from Great Britain.

In 1896 the New York state legislator passed a statute requiring a license to perform audits and use the title Certified Public Accountant (CPA). Existing accountants were grandfathered under the act. The first two to become CPAs without taking the certification exam were Frank Broaker and Charles Haskins from the firm Haskins and Sells. The first person to pass the CPA examination was a university professor from NYU, Joseph Hardcastle. The first woman to pass the examination was Christine Ross in 1898. Other states followed suit and passed similar legislation. The current CPA examination is uniform in all states and therefore provides for reciprocity when a CPA moves to a different state. Reciprocity between states is not available to attorneys. They must retake the bar exam if they move out of the state in which they passed the exam. But then the pass rate on the bar in Pennsylvania is over 90% where as the pass rate on the CPA exam is right at 20%. That is because a curve is applied to candidate's scores to raise the rate to exactly 20%.

Two other noteworthy events during this era; one was the creation of "The Journal of Accountancy" in 1905. Accountants are blessed with one journal that does it all for the profession. The second event was the adoption of accrual accounting method by the Internal Revenue Service in 1909.

THE GREAT DEPRESSION

The causes of the great depression are complex involving the role of interest rates and the application of the gold standard, but the resulting harsh realities of depression life made Americans question capitalism and even democracy. The nation transitioned from a laissez-faire economy to one that became highly regulated. For the financial community, the accounting profession and the services offered, financial statements took center stage. This marked the initial recognition of the extreme importance for the use of reliable financial statements (annual reports), a product that is now created by a combination of GAAP and GAAS. In order to sell securities to the general public, a company was now required to register with the Securities and Exchange Commission (SEC) and follow the rules outlined in GAAP and GAAS (or what the accounting profession calls attestation). Both GAAP and GAAS emerged from the accounting profession's national organization, back then it was called the American Institute of Accountants. The name changed in 1957, to become the American Institute of Certified Public Accountants or AICPA. GAAP was the specific responsibility of a subcommittee called the Accounting Principles Board or APB. Most current GAAP pronouncements will reference the early work done by the APB.

The unscrupulous behavior exhibited during the great depression demonstrated the need for some type of governance and control. The governmental agency created to protect the financial investor called itself the Security and Exchange Commission or SEC. The Securities Acts of 1933 and 1934 set the ground rules for financial statement disclosure, the trading of securities and corporate registration. They still oversee the laws that are in effect today to regulate the securities industry. One of the primary functions of the SEC is to disclose financial information on publicly held companies in a standardized format. The service they provide to do this is called EDGAR, short for Electronic Data Gathering, Analysis, and Retrieval system. It can be found at: http://www.sec.gov/edgar.shtml.

The following list illustrates the types of disclosures required by the SEC; the system is called the Integrated Disclosure System (IDS):

S1 – This is the registration of an Initial Public Offering (IPO) and requires extensive disclosure including three years of audited financial statements. The SEC will respond in 60 days to the filing of an S1. The sixty days is referred to as the "quiet period" when the company just waits for the SEC to respond.

S2 – Somewhat limited disclosure, but still a significant burden on the company to provide detailed information.

S3 – Limited information and forms. For companies already in compliance but who want to make an additional public offering.

The following list illustrates the names of the SEC forms listed on EDGAR:

Form 10-K is the annual report due 90 days after year-end.

Form 10-Q is the quarterly report due 45 days after the end of the quarter.

Form 8-K is a current report triggered by an event due 15 days after the event.

FASB

The next major event in accounting history was the creation of the Financial Accounting Standards Board or FASB in 1973. The perceived problem was a lack of uniformed practices and the application of standardized rules among the AICPA. The eight largest multinational accounting firms totally dominated the AICPA. So the application of GAAP always favored their largest clients. The big eight audited about 98% of the publicly traded companies. The big eight accounting firms at that time were as follows: Arthur Andersen, Coopers and Lybrand, Deloitte Haskins and Sells, Ernst and Whinney, Peat Marwick Mitchell, Price Waterhouse, Touche Ross, and Arthur Young. Non-public companies did not use the big eight accounting firms for auditing services because they did not need the prestige of the big eight to sell shares to the public. These companies complained to their Congressperson that they lacked representation in the formulation of GAAP. The AICPA ignored the complaints, forcing Congress to create the FASB, giving it responsibility for the establishment of GAAP for both public and non-public companies. (It must be noted that from a legal perspective, the SEC has always held the final (veto) authority for the formation and enforcement of GAAP.) There is a similar agency for governmental GAAP called the Governmental Accounting Standards Board. This did not, however, stop the criticism toward the big eight accounting firms. Two governmental reports, the Metcalf report in 1977 and the Cohen Commission Report in 1978, were extremely critical of the audit process. GAAS was now also under attack!

PRESENT DAY CRISIS (ENRON & WORLDCOM)

The unthinkable happened, Enron, a company thought to be too large to go bankrupt, filed for bankruptcy. This bankruptcy was followed by a second company, WorldCom, the largest in U.S. history. The bankruptcy of Enron in December 2001 (62 billion in assets) and WorldCom in July 2002 (100 billion in assets) attracted nationwide attention. The Accounting Profession was the assumed political target for financial irresponsibility. The publicity was very negative. There was a significant loss of confidence in accountants, public and private. The same firm, Arthur Andersen, then one of the big five, audited both companies. The financial statements of these two companies proved grossly misleading to investors, creditors and lending institutions. Lots of finger pointing resulted, to include a sharp criticism of GAAP.

What happened? Enron actually played a very simple game by creatively manipulating nebulous accounting rules. They would purchase an asset for 10 million and then sell it to a Special Purpose Entity (SPE) they controlled for 12 million, recognizing 2 million in profit. Unfortunately, the SPE financed the purchase with debt, guaranteed by Enron. However, during consolidaton, the SPE activity, according to accounting rules were not required to rollup into the parent company's financial statements, although there was a requirement to disclose the debt. These sales occurred on the daily basis, inflating the reported profits of Enron without disclosure of the debt guarantee by the parent company, a clear violation of the rules of disclosure. Posting billions in revenue from the sale of assets inflated profits and earned Enron a ranking of 7th in the fortune 500. The accounting tricks pleased Wall Street analyst until the truth was discovered. The founder, Kenneth Lay and the ex-CEO Jeffrey Skilling pocked millions from the inflated share price.[4]

PCAOB

The answer to the problem (by the U.S. Congress) was the passage of the Sarbanes-Oxley Act (SOX), signed into legislation on 30 July 2002. The provisions of the Act applied to both publicly held companies and their audit firms. A major provision of the Act required the creation of the Public Company Accounting Oversight Board (PCAOB). The role of the PCAOB is to "provide oversight for auditors of public companies, including establishing auditing and quality control standards for public company audits."[5] The PCAOB now performs inspections of the quality controls at

[4] Hays, Kristen, Associated Press, Philadelphia Inquirer, January 22, 2006. At the point in time this chapter was written, the trial for Lay and Skilling had not begun. The trial was scheduled for January 30, 2006.

[5] Holtzman, Yair, Journal of Management Development Volume 23 Number 10 2004 pp. 949-961 Copyright © Emerald Group Publishing Limited ISSN 0262-1711

audit firms under their supervision. Last year this function was performed at the peer review level (firm to firm). The Act employs a host of rules that auditors and corporate management must (struggle) comply with to evaluate the existence and effectiveness of the control environment, as well as the fair presentation of financial statements. In fact, every audit now results in the issuance of three opinions: one opinion on the evaluation of management assessment of the corporate control environment, one opinion on the effectiveness of the control environment and the final opinion on the fair presentation of financial statements. In addition, the AICPA also responded in 2002 with the Statement on Auditing Standards No 99, Consideration of Fraud in a Financial Statement Audit. The statement was intended to provide expanded detection guidance to auditors, but the train had already departed the station! GAAS now belongs to the PCAOB, not the AICPA for publicly traded companies.

The following is a brief sample summary of the Sarbanes-Oxley Act as provided by the AICPA regarding auditing standards or GAAS.

http://www.aicpa.org/info/sarbanes_oxley_summary.htm

Section 103: Auditing, Quality Control, And Independence Standards And Rules.

The (PCAOB) Board shall:

(1) register public accounting firms;

(2) establish, or adopt, by rule, "auditing, quality control, ethics, independence, and other standards relating to the preparation of audit reports for issuers;"

(3) conduct inspections of accounting firms;

(4) conduct investigations and disciplinary proceedings, and impose appropriate sanctions;

(5) perform such other duties or functions as necessary or appropriate;

(6) enforce compliance with the Act, the rules of the Board, professional standards, and the securities laws relating to the preparation and issuance of audit reports and the obligations and liabilities of accountants with respect thereto;

(7) set the budget and manage the operations of the Board and the staff of the Board.

Auditing standards. The Board would be required to "cooperate on an on-going basis" with designated professional groups of accountants and any advisory groups convened in connection with standard-setting, and although the Board can "to the extent that it determines appropriate" adopt standards proposed by those groups, the Board will have authority to amend, modify, repeal, and reject any standards suggested by the groups. The Board must report on its standard-setting activity to the Commission on an annual basis.

CAPITAL MARKETS, MACRO VIEW

It is all about money and trust. Capital Markets link corporate savings to great business ideas through Financial Intermediaries such as investment bankers, venture capitalists, mutual funds, bankers and individual traders. Financial reporting plays a crucial role in the decision-making and performance of capital markets. Accounting and auditing provides the information that drives the system, or what might be called the decision making of "Information

Intermediaries." Everyone in the investment community uses financial accounting information (financial analysts, bond-rating agencies, the financial press) all with the same goal, to assist investors in distinguishing between great investment opportunities and poor ones. Businesses conduct economic transactions on a perpetual cycle while accounting records are periodically summarized into financial statements. The rule that drives the formation of these financial statements is accrual accounting, the hallmark of GAAP.

Contrary to popular opinion, there is some flexibility in the application of GAAP. The decision on how to apply GAAP is determined by senior management at the company level with the consent of external auditors. The big eight are now down to a big four after a host of mergers: PriceWaterhouseCoopers, Ernst & Young, KPMG and Deloitte & Touche. Andersen received a felony conviction for their part in the Enron scandal resulting in the dissolution of their partnership in the summer of 2002. All of the remaining firms are enormous in scale, auditing almost all of the publicly held companies but they still remain just as volatile as Andersen. Each of the big four accounting firms will recruit thousands of college graduates each year, searching for those who excel in majored concentrations of accounting, finance and information technology.

CAPITAL MARKETS, MICRO VIEW

At the company level, management has broad powers to determine how GAAP is applied and used to measure company assets and net income (or what investors call the bottom line). Auditors, on the other hand, seek to constrain the application of GAAP to common industry practices and norms. Conservative accounting is not "good" accounting.[6] Company management possesses superior information about the financial position of their company and this information should be accurately and fairly reflected in their financial statements. Auditors may take conservative positions to limit their legal exposure for opportunistic misrepresentation. This means setting limits on management's ability to misuse accounting judgments (estimates), hence the basis of most conflicts between management and auditors. It must also be acknowledged that management is highly motivated to present the best possible financial position and financial performance of the company. Here is a short list of management incentives:

1. Management compensation is often based on performance. Only one million dollars of salary is tax deductible to a U.S. corporation. This means that compensation above one million must come from employee share options. For example, imagine that the option is to purchase #200,000 shares at $25.00/share, given to the CEO when the shares are selling for $20.00/share. The option lasts for two years. The CEO will exercise the Internal Revenue Code section 83(b) election, which allows the value of the option to be recognized for tax purposes when received. The tax on receipt of the options is zero because anything less than zero in an income tax calculation is zero $(20 - 25 = 0)$

[6] Palepu, Healy & Bernard, Business Analysis and Valuation, 3e, Using Financial Statements, Thomson, Southwestern, 2004, page 3-11.

and therefore the subsequent exercise of the options is not a taxable event under section 83(b). If the CEO can raise the share price to $45.00, in a significant way, from the production of favorable financial statements, the gain in compensation will be four million dollars $(45 - 25)*(200,000) = 4$ million. Greed is a powerful motivator and should never be underestimated.

2. Bond covenants are based on financial statements. Violation of debt covenants is a serious event and to be avoided at all cost. Even in the nonprofit sector, bond ratings are a strong incentive to produce favorable financial statements.

3. Keeping shareholders satisfied is a primary function of the CEO and CFO. If the board of directors perceives that the company needs a turnaround to produce profit, the top management will be looking for new jobs. All of these decisions are based on the financial accounting numbers.

GAAP FLEXIBILITY:

What are some of the more common variations of GAAP application available to management to manipulate the financial accounting results? Note, flexibility refers to choosing an accounting policy is most often industry specific and favorable:

1. The most frequently used policy to manipulate earnings is the timing of revenue recognition. GAAP provides for significant lead-way in

making this decision. In some industries, it is commonplace to recognize earnings when a sale is made rather than the more tradition method of when the goods are shipped. This was a common practice for Oracle Corporation until Wall Street's down grading of the shares forced the Board of Directors to change the CEO and the accounting policies. (Of course holding the books open several extra weeks to report sales, but not expenses, will also have a positive impact on the bottom line. This is not GAAP but a common practice in some retail industries.)

2. Accounting estimates regarding the life of fixed assets. There are standards published in the Asset Class Life Range book, but these are not fixed rules. Doubling the life of an asset will cut the depreciation expense in half.

3. Depreciation methods. The difference between double declining balance and the straight-line method is very significant.

4. Setting a low minimum capitalization policy. Some companies will capitalize amounts as small as $500 and others will expense the purchase of fixed assets up to $5,000. The deciding factor is often the materiality threshold, which makes this as an audit issues. The cumulative affect of this policy can be very significant. If the goal is to lower earnings to provide smoothing or avoid the purchase of fixed assets, large purchases can

also be ordered in separate parts to stay under the threshold so that all of it can be expensed.[7] This should be a violation of the company's internal control policies. If the company has an internal auditor, the practice of purchasing a large asset in small units might be caught internally. It was common practice at AOL to book the expense of mass mailing computer disks to prospective customers as an asset called "Subscriber Acquisition Costs" which they held for eighteen months before amortizing it.

5. Inventory methods. FIFO will create lower expenses in Cost of Goods Sold than LIFO if input prices are rising. The problem is that the inventory method for financial accounting must match that of the income tax return (IRS Form 1120). A switch requires support from the public accounting firm in the form a letter and approval from the Internal Revenue Service.

6. Expense estimates for items such as the allowance for uncollectibles. This is always a hot spot between auditors and management.

7. Then there are the creative games like outsourcing research with a special purpose entity (SPE), when the activity never leaves the facilities of the company. The creation of special purpose entities can certainly be

---

[7] This is particularly true in African nations that tax based on fixed assets instead of net earnings.

useful as a means of limiting risk. They are frequently used in the drug industry to limit the risk on the development of a new drug. This creates the opportunity for a new set of investors (shareholders in the SPE) who are willing to accept a higher level of risk.

8. Accounting for the write-down of goodwill. Under FASB rules the auditor is responsible for the evaluation of the fair market value assigned to goodwill by company management created as a result of past mergers.

9. Policies regarding the recognition of pension liability (if appropriate) and the assumptions used by the actuary to determine pension liability. Does the company disclose under-funded pension plans? Factors involve the expected return on plan assets and the rate of increase in wages and healthcare costs.

AUDITOR AND INVESTOR RESPONSIBILITY

The flip side to management's flexibility is the responsibility of the auditor and the investor to examine the company's financial statements to determine management's fair presentation of financial activity. Below is a list of basic analytical techniques. Please note this list is not exhaustive by any means. Every great auditor has a number of techniques at their disposal:

1. A great place to begin is to determine if the company has issued pro-forma financial statements or a letter by the CEO prior to year-

end, promising a specific earnings objective. If these exist, the company's financial accounting team may be under some pressure to hit the projections. This is commonly referred to as the smoothing of earnings.

2. Check to see if the accounting policies of the company being examined are consistent with industry norms. It might be discovered that the company is the "best of breed" and are setting the pace for others to follow. If however, their assets are estimated to last 20 years and the industry standard is ten, there could be an underlying attempt by senior management to manipulate earnings. Always be open to alternative explanations! Different is not necessarily bad!

3. Does management hold significant outstanding options on shares? Again, check common industry practice. Greed is a powerful motivator. It is not uncommon for options to make-up the majority of the CEO's compensation package. This is not necessarily a bad thing. In fact, it is commonplace for the CEO to hold millions of dollars worth of options, but does the CEO exercise influence over accounting in such a manner as to inflate earnings?

4. Check the compliance with debt covenants. If the ability to borrow additional funds is dependant on a strong earnings report, management has a strong incentive to "dress up" the financial statements.

5. Watch for unexplained changes in accounting estimates, estimates that are highly judgmental and lacking in supporting documentation or non-cash transactions designed specifically to improve earnings. For example, a debt for equity swap can create a paper gain.

6. Changes in accounting principles should be clearly disclosed. Is the disclosure adequate for a knowledgeable reader? Is the change reasonable? The change from LIFO to FIFO will often create "inventory profit" as the accounting records reflect the sale of old, less expensive inventory, which only exists in the accounting records. This gain cannot be avoided, but was the motivation for the change, increased earnings? Timing becomes a key element in the analysis.

7. The gap in the cash flow from operations compared to net income will be affected by the amount of depreciation and inventory necessary for expansion into new stores. The investment in new equipment will lower net income through depreciation but increase the cash flow from operations as it is added back. The investment in additional inventory will decrease cash flow from operations and not impact net income. Therefore, the gap between cash flow from operations and net income will both increase and decrease over time. It should not always be increasing unless the company is in a period of rapid expansion.

8. The percentage relationship of accounts receivable to sales should be studied. A desperate company will increase sales by opening the door to non-creditworthy customers. The uncollectibles account should start to increase as percentage of accounts receivables. Because accounts receivable is always presented as a net number, it is necessary to add back the allowance account before making the percentage calculation. A dishonest manager might record fictitious sales to boost profits; this will also increase accounts receivables to sales.

9. Always remember that the best method to hide expenses is to classify them as assets, both are debit entries. This was the sin of WorldCom; they booked expenses as assets. When the top management of PharMor Pharmacy decided to boost profits, they booked expenses as cookies. Their inventory showed millions of dollars in cookies and the auditor did not question the balance until PharMor filed for bankruptcy.

10. Always review variable expenses as a percentage of revenue. Expenses should increase proportionately to revenue. Management will need to explain fluctuations that reflect their knowledge of the business rather than regurgitate recorded activity in their general ledger account. For example, significant <u>decreases</u> in fuel expense to operate machinery and equipment in a manufacturing environment

does not make sense if there is a significant increase in revenues due to new customer sales. However, it will make sense if the company purchased fuel at a lower cost in a prior period using hedge contracts.

11. Review large and non recurring journal entries; also include the topside journal entries that are posted at the end of the period. Many times unscrupulous management practices attempt to classify short-term commitments as long term positions to make their balance sheet look more attractive.

12. The list is endless depending on access to the records. For example, an auditor might check for large fourth-quarter adjustments as the company seeks to adjust pro-forma data with audited data. Auditors will also know if the company has been "opinion shopping" by playing accounting firms against each other. Related-party transactions are always suspect. This was the downfall of the KrispyKreme Doughnut Company. Investors seldom have access to this kind of information but sometimes-even auditors will miss finding related party transactions.

CONCLUSION

What is the bottom line for the accounting profession as a result of the shift in control of GAAP & GAAS and public perceptions of accountants? It is clear that the financial community and governmental agencies are demanding more from accountants: more honesty, greater understanding of business processes and increased fraud detection procedures. The scandals has also created an unusual public reaction, it has smashed the old perception of accounting as being dull and boring. Suddenly accountants are called upon to be detectives and forensic investigators ready to provide insight into fraudulent financial activity and wrongdoing. Some reporters claim that it made accounting "sexy."[8] One thing is certain, it has increased the demand for qualified accountants and the competition is pushing up wages![9] What better time than now, for Christians who have trained themselves to resist the temptation and seduction of wealth, to become auditors, controllers and chief financial officers? It is all about being trustworthy with worldly wealth. Consider the wisdom of the words of Jesus for our modern society:

> [10]*"Whoever can be trusted with very little can also be trusted with much, and whoever is dishonest with very little will also be dishonest with much.* [11]*So if you have not been trustworthy in handling worldly wealth, who will trust you with true riches?* [12]*And if you have not been trustworthy with someone else's property, who will give you property of your own?* [13]*"No servant can serve two masters. Either he will hate the one and love the other, or he will be devoted to the one and despise the other. You cannot serve both God and Money."*

---

[8] Shepard, Scott, philadelphia.bizjournals.com, August 5-11, 2005.
[9] Von Bergen, Jane, The Philadelphia Inquirer, October 12, 2005, D1.

PART II –
Accounting's
Spiritual Roots

Chapter 3

HEAVENLY ACCOUNTING ~

GOD'S ACCOUNTING SYSTEM REVEALED THROUGH THE SCRIPTURES

By
Dr. Jack E. Bower
Eastern University

INTRODUCTION

No human being can comprehend the majesty and wisdom of God. Does a perfect God with an infallible memory keep a general ledger? Of course not, but just like the "streets of gold" God uses the imagery of keeping books to help us understand His relationship with mankind. "Heavenly Accounting" gives some insight into how God would do it if, in fact, God did keep books in the way that we finite humans understand double-entry accounting.

The entity concept is the first struggle of using the scriptural references to accounting terminology. The scriptures were written from God's perspective, and therefore; the accounting references are to God's accounting equation. Abraham's faith (credit) reduced his accounts receivable. We want to read the scriptures from the perspective of their own spiritual accounting equation. In an individual (entity) equation, perhaps faith would be the owner's equity and the fruits of the spirit would be the assets.

JUSTICE AND LOVE

The God of the Christian faith is a God of justice and love. Justice means God must punish sin. Love is His desire to forgive us. These two qualities present a dilemma for a perfect God when establishing a contractual relationship with a less than perfect mankind. God didn't create the universe with this paradox. The dilemma or impasse in the relationship was a result of mankind's violation of specific provisions of God's covenant with them (Gen. 2:16,17). The details of the violation are described in Genesis chapter three. Here is a brief outline from an accounting perspective.

ASSETS = GRACE

When God created the world it was a perfect place free of intentional irregularities, and God could freely interact with His creation in a mode of love. The accounting equation was simply; the assets of heaven and earth = the grace of God, His net worth in creation. Mankind, through interaction with God's major competitor Satan, broke the terms of the contract with God the Creator. Mankind was forced to vacate the premises of Eden and to enter a less than desirable work environment.

"Cursed is the ground because of you; through painful toil you will eat of it all the days of your life. It will produce thorns and thistles for you and you will eat the plants of the field. By the sweat of your brow you will eat your food until you return to the ground since from it you were taken;" Gen. 3:17ff

The eviction notice was not sufficient restitution for the intentional violation on the part of mankind. This violation meant that the status of mankind with God changed. God reclassified man from the most significant part of the inventory of creation "God created man in his own image" (Gen. 1:27), to an accounts receivable. After the reclassification, mankind was now accountable for every minor violation; even every careless word spoken is charged to an account for each member of humanity (Matt 12:36). With mankind's violation of the contract a new element entered the accounting equation, "sin", a liability account for God to repay. Equating sin with debt is well documented in the scriptures. In the words of Jesus "Forgive us our debts as we also have forgiven our debtors" Matthew 6:12.

ASSETS = SIN + GRACE

*The Lord replied to Moses. Whoever has sinned against me I will blot out of my **book***...*
However when the time comes for me to punish, I will punish them for their sins."
Exodus 32:33f

*"But I tell you that men will have to give **account** on the day of judgment for every careless word they have spoken."* Matthew 12:36

"So then, each of us will give an account of himself to God." Romans 14:12

"And I saw the dead, great and small, standing before the throne, and books were opened. Another book was opened, which is the book of life.* The dead were judged according to what they had done as recorded in the books." Revelation 20:12

> **SIDEBAR - Notice that there are two ledgers for humanity's accounts receivable. One special or subsidiary ledger is the "Book of Life" and the other is simply called "The Books". (More about this point later.)*

Back to the two qualities of God, justice and love. This is the dilemma for God. The justice quality of God required a proper payment for the violation of the contract called sin, but the love quality of God wants to forgive the violation and interact freely with mankind. Of course, the violations have continued in an exponential manner as mankind has multiplied and treated each other wrongly and therefore sinned against God.

Does mankind earn any credits against each individual account receivable? Yes, God is compared to a king who wants to settle the accounts of His servants (Matt 18:23ff). The story told by Jesus concerns a debtor who is forgiven a large debt but is unwilling to forgive even a small debt owed to him. As each person forgives the debt of others they establish credit with God against the debits of their violations (James 5:20).

The journal entry for sin:

	Dr.	Cr.
Accounts Receivable	XXX	
Sin		XXX

The journal entry for good deeds and forgiveness of others:

Grace	XXX	
Accounts Receivable		XXX

Can good deeds and good thoughts fully repay the accounts receivable of each person? This key question was the principle subject of two books by the apostle Paul: Romans and Galatians. (These were best sellers of their times.) In these books, Paul argues very effectively that no one can be declared paid in full by human deeds alone. Paul uses the example of Abraham, who was the father of their nation and known as an extremely righteous man. In other words, if the person with the greatest good deeds and good thoughts in Jewish history couldn't do it, than no one can. It was the **faith** of Abraham that was **credited** to his account, not his good deeds (Gen. 15:6).

The journal entry for Abraham's faith was:

	Dr.	Cr.
Grace	XXX	
Accounts Receivable		XXX

Many faith groups argue that it is a Biblical principle that good deeds cover sin. Therefore, faithful church attendance will score some points with God; sort of like punching a spiritual time clock.

Interestingly, certain good deeds will even cover a multitude of sins.

"Remember this: Whoever turns a sinner from the error of his way will save him from death and cover over a multitude of sins." James 5:20.

The key question is this. Are good deeds enough to pay for ALL sin? Does a just God need to punish mankind who has more debits than credits? The answer is YES! The most convincing story of the principle that good deeds are never enough is told by Jesus in Matt 19. A wealthy young man comes to Jesus and asks what is necessary for eternal life. Jesus gives him the check list: Thou shall not... Certainly Jesus thought he would get the point, but he did not. "All these I have kept", the young man said. "What do I still lack?". Okay Jesus said, "If you want to be perfect, go sell your possessions and give to the poor, and you will have treasure in heaven. Then come, follow me." The man left very sad because he had substantial investments. The disciples asked, "Who then can be saved?" Jesus looked at them and said. *"With man this is impossible, but with God all things are possible."* Matthew 19:16ff

How was God going to reconcile the books and draw man back to Himself? This was a complex problem in logic that even Satan couldn't unravel until it actually happened. God, who wants to forgive the debits, can't because of His basic quality of justice. Mankind wants to have the account paid but can't earn enough credits to justify the account.

How God would solve this dilemma was the greatest mystery story of all time, one that baffled Jewish theologians and Satan for centuries (Eph. 3:5).

God's answer was to have the accounts of humanity cleared by a transfer to the account of someone without sin. Someone with so large a credit balance that the debits of all of humanity couldn't wipe out that balance. Jesus Christ was the answer, a mystery hidden throughout the centuries. Here was the perfect person who could become sin for all of mankind, thereby reconciling God to mankind.

How did Jesus obtain so large a credit balance? Did Jesus have a credit balance as a result of His involvement in creation?

"Through him all things were made; without him nothing was made that has been made." John 1:3

	Dr.	Cr.
Heaven and Earth	XXX	
Jesus Christ		XXX

Did this credit balance stay with Him as he was reclassified from Godhead to a part of humanity? This is an interesting accounting question. This passage in Phil 2:6 would argue no, but the passage in Col. 2:9 would argue yes.

"Who, being in very nature God, did not consider equality with God something to be grasped, but made himself nothing, taking the very nature of a servant, being made in human likeness." Phil 2:6f

"For in Christ all the fullness of the Deity lives in bodily form." Col. 2:9

	Dr.	Cr.
Jesus Christ (Humanity)	XXX	
Jesus Christ (Grace)		XXX

The above two journals are just food for thought. The true source of the inexhaustible Credit on the account of Jesus Christ came from His willingness to suffer and die on the cross. On the cross a sinless man becomes sin for all of humanity. The justice quality of God required him to turn his head, as His own son died a slow and painful death.

> *"My God, my God, why have you forsaken me?"* Matt 27:46

The credit was so significant that it even covered the debits of those who lived and died before the death of Jesus (Heb 10:1-10).

The good news of the gospel is that an accounting transfer is now available to all of humanity. A transfer that removes the debit balance and even results in a reclassification from the regular ledger to the subsidiary ledger called the Book of Life. Those in the book of life are still charged with sin, but if you are listed in the book of life the blood of Jesus Christ continually removes your debit balance.

> *"But if we walk in the light, as He is in the light, we have fellowship with one another, and the blood of Jesus, his Son, purifies us from all sin."* I John 1:7

What does it cost to receive this soul saving transfer? The price is free, if you name Jesus Lord of your life!

"For it is by grace you have been saved, through faith - and this is not from yourselves, it is the gift of God - not by works, so that no one can boast." Ephesians 2:8

Jesus is our Jubilee. The forgiveness of debt God wanted for His people as outlined in Leviticus 25 was finally fulfilled by Jesus on the cross. (Luke 4:21) Now that is GOOD NEWS!

"The spirit of the Lord is on me, because he has anointed me to preach good news to the poor. He has sent me to proclaim freedom for the prisoners and recovery of sight for the blind, to release the oppressed, and <u>to proclaim the year of the Lord's favor.</u>"

Chapter 4

ACCOUNTING'S SAINTLY ANCESTRY

THE INFLUENCE OF SAINT THOMAS AQUINAS ON DOUBLE ENTRY ACCOUNTING

By
Dr. Jack E. Bower, CPA
Associate Professor of Accounting
Eastern University

Was double-entry accounting divinely inspired? At least one Scholar thinks so. Professor Jack Bower from Eastern University believes double-entry accounting was inspired by the dual nature of God, revealed in the Holy Scriptures, as understood by Saint Thomas Aquinas. According to Professor Bower it is only a matter of following the clues back to the inspiration provided by Saint Thomas Aquinas. This chapter builds the rational for the hypothesis that Saint Thomas Aquinas or one of his immediate disciples formulated the system now known as double-entry accounting and the Balance Sheet equation. This article will show proximity, location, timing, motive and opportunity on the part of this great theologian to address the issue of bookkeeping and creation of the balance sheet based on the dual nature of God. Unfortunately, this time period is the most *"neglected chapter in the history of economics."*[1] It has been described as the Commercial Revolution that led to the Industrial Revolution. Records from this time period are difficult to obtain and study.

DEFINITION OF THE TERM DOUBLE ENTRY ACCOUNTING:

Accounting records comprise some of the earliest written documents known to mankind such as the clay tokens found in Mesopotamia that were used as the first bills of lading.[2] Accounting records and reports were developed in the Islamic State beginning in 622 and continued to advance during the development of the Muslim religion.[3] The recording of two sides of a transaction as opposites to one another contains a key element of double entry, but remains a single-entry system until an effort is made to balance the debits against the credits. Most accounting historians accept this definition. The critical question is when did the transition occur from recording each side of a transaction (single entry) into a self-balancing set of accounts (double entry)? There are several theories and

[1] Chafuen, Alejandro A., <u>Faith and Liberty, The Economic Thought of the Late Scholastics,</u> Lexington Books, Lanham Maryland, 2003, page 7

[2] *"The Roots of Writing,"* Time, August 1, 1977, page 76.

[3] Zaid, Omar Abdullah. *"Were Islamic Records Precursors to Accounting Books Based on the Italian Method?"* Accounting Historians Journal, Vol 27, No. 1, June 2000. page 87.

as one author has observed: *"Students of the subject, in an endeavor to give due credit for the invention of the system, offer a wide range of possibilities."*[4] This chapter offers yet another plausible explanation for the invention of double-entry accounting.

FIRST CLUE: TIMING

For English readers, Professor Geoffrey A. Lee from the University of Nottingham is our renowned scholar of ancient accounting documents from this time period. The historical references in this section are from several of his works.[5] The problem is that parchment was scarce and accounting records were seldom preserved. Most accounting historians agree that the oldest know record of the recording of transactions with opposing entries is the Florentine Bank Ledger Fragments of 1211.

In the 1211 ledger, there is no effort to balance the accounts of this banking partnership.[6] One theory is that this was a double-entry system, but the balancing portions of the ledger were lost. Another theory is that this ledger combined with other private ledgers being separately maintained would produce a self-balancing set of books.[7] Professor Lee believes that there is strong argument for this hypothesis. Unfortunately, the

---

[4] Edward Pergallo, Origin and Evolution of Double Entry Bookkeeping, A Study of Italian Practice from the Fourteenth Century, American Institute Publishing Company, 1939, page 1.

[5] *Journal of Accounting Research*, Spring 1973, 47-61 & *Abacus*, December 1973, 137-155 & *Nottingham Medieval Studies*, Vol XVI, 1972, pages 28-60.

[6] Geoffrey A. Lee, The Florentine Bank Ledger Fragments of 1211, Journal of Accounting Research, Spring 1973, page 47-61.

[7] Geoffrey Lee, Abacus, December 1979, pages 148ff.

additional ledgers have never been found to validate this theory.

The oldest surviving record of a valid double-entry accounting system is the ledger of Reniere Fini & Brothers of 1296 to 1305 and the Giovanni Farolfi & Company of 1299 to 1300.[8] Both of these ledgers were self-balancing with a capital account to record the difference between revenue and expense. These accounts show debits and credits in opposition to each other, not simply two parts of the same transaction. The partners' capital account is the algebraic sum of the difference between assets and liabilities. The concept of an accounting period was also starting to develop.[9]

The critical question is what happened between 1211 and 1296? What causes the algebraic breakthrough in bookkeeping? What created the idea of setting things equal to each other? What was the critical intellectual influence of this time period? The answer is quite obvious; Saint Thomas Aquinas lived from 1226 to 1274. *"He was the foremost Scholastic writer. His influence was so widespread that nearly all subsequent Schoolmen studied, quoted, and commented upon his remarks."*[10] This is the first clue, the timing was perfect.

[8] Some historians argue that the ledger of the "Massari of the Commune of Genoa" dated 1340 is the first complete example of a double entry accounting system. See: Edward Peragallo, Origins and evolution of double entry bookkeeping, 1938, page 3.
[9] Geoffrey A. Lee, The coming of age of double entry: The Giovanni Farolfi ledger of 1299-1300, The Accounting Historians Journal, Fall 1977, page 51.
[10] Chafuen, Alejandro A., Faith and Liberty, The Economic Thought of the Late Scholastics, Lexington Books, Lanham Maryland, 2003, page 14.

SECOND CLUE: FATHER OF THE CONSERVATION EQUATION

Most scholars in the Natural Sciences credit Saint Thomas Aquinas as being the first mathematician to use the conservation equation. This equation is a principle in physics to show relationships equal to each other and was a part of his five ways to prove that God exists.[11] The Balance Sheet is a good example of a conservation equation. Another example would be Einstein's E=mc2. It is strange that all most every description of the historical development of physics will include a brief mention of the contribution by Saint Thomas Aquinas and the yet the theological community refuses to acknowledge his contribution to the field of mathematics or physics. The second clue to the hypothesis is that he is accepted as the father of the conservation equation, and the balance sheet: Assets = Liabilities + Owners Equity is a good example of this equation.

THIRD CLUE: MOTIVE

Medieval society consisted of a feudal economy bound together by tradition. Each estate or kingdom was a complete economic unit capable of supplying all of its physical needs. The lords were given use of the land by the king and they in turn allocated the land to their serfs. The serfs paid the lords in crops or labor and the lords paid the king in crops or money. To not accept the system was rebellion against God.[12] To

[11] Wulf, Maurice, The Philosophical System of Thomas Aquinas, http://radicalacademy.com/philaquinasmdw16.htm

[12] "Everyone must submit himself to the governing authorities, for there is no authority except that which God has established. The authorities that exist have been established by God. Consequently, he who rebels against the authority is rebelling against what God has instituted, and those who do so will bring judgment on themselves." Romans 13:1-2 NIV.

change the system was opposition to the will of God. But change did take place as technology and other forces began to erode and disrupt the feudal economic system.

The forces of change were addressed by several monks who attempted to prescribe rules of economic conduct compatible with religious doctrine. "The most important of the scholastic writers was St. Thomas Aquinas."[13] The key issue was the ownership of private property. The allocation of scarce resources by price created issues of equity and justice which St. Thomas Aquinas focused upon.[14] Aquinas concluded that making a reasonable profit from a "just price" was not a sin because it was a reasonable means of meeting the needs of the trading parties. Saint Thomas mentioned the following as justification of profits:

To provide for the businessman's household

To help the poor.

To ensure that the country does not run short of essential supplies.

To compensate the businessman's work.

To improve the merchandise.[15]

The calculation of a "just profit" required an accounting system. This is why the Church was so involved in distribution of the first

[13] Harry Landreth & David Colander, History of Economic Thought, Houghton Mifflin Company, Princeton N.J. 1994, page 30.

[14] William Benton, Publisher, Biographical Note, St. Thomas Aquinas, The Summa Theologica, Vol I, Encyclopedia Britannica, Inc., 1952. "Thomas between 1265 and 1269 commented on the Physics, Metaphysics, On the Soul, Ethics, Politics, and the Posterior Analytics." page vi.

[15] Chafuen, Alejandro A., Faith and Liberty, The Economic Thought of the Late Scholastics, Lexington Books, Lanham Maryland, 2003, page 115.

accounting system, to reduce sin. Aquinas' meeting of human needs was based upon Aristotle's conception of need. In general, Aquinas "advanced economics and all the social sciences by his use of abstract thinking."[16]

"Thomas Aquinas' Summa Theologiae reconciled reason and religion, completed the integration of the classical learning and the Christian theology, and remains to this day the basis of all Catholic theological teaching."[17]

Construction of cities, castles and cathedrals created wealth. Logic and legalism were needed to rule and manage the affairs of men. Accounting for inventory and a fair profit became an issue. Max Weber believed that *"the development of double-entry book-keeping".. "was a phenomenon of major importance in opening the way for the regularizing of capitalistic enterprise."[18]*

In general, a spirit of optimism and self-satisfaction was widespread, encouraged by rising material prosperity. Of course, prosperity was metal kitchenware and candles for the poor. For the rich, prosperity was fine wall hangings and bed furnishings or chests with hinges and locks. The wealthy could even afford windows of glass in their homes.[19] It is hard for people in modern societies to appreciate the desperate need for reason and logic in the Middle Ages.

[16] Harry Landreth & David Colander, History of Economic Thought, page 32.

[17] William Langer, Editor; An Encyclopedia of World History, 4th Edition, Houghton Mifflin Company, Boston, 1968, page 247.

[18] Giddens, Anthony. Introduction to "The Protestant Ethic and the Spirit of Capitalism" by Max Weber, page 8.

[19] Norman Kotker editor, Morris Bishop author, Middle Ages, American Heritage Pub. Co. Inc. 1968, page 37.

Superstitions ruled the day. For example, relics such as bones were of extreme importance. The bones of famous persons were a major commodity of exchange and some feared that they were more valuable dead, as bones, than alive. When Saint Thomas Aquinas died his body was decapitated and boiled in the monastery of Fossanuova in order to keep his bones.[20] Logic and reason were scarce commodities and St. Thomas Aquinas was the major provider of a voice of reason during these transitional times.

The Education of St. Thomas Aquinas: Dominic of Caleruega in Spain was a devoted friend and ally of Saint Francis. He was a scholar and an excellent administrator. His goal was a higher academy in the greater monasteries and a kind of graduate school in the major cities. He established a school in Paris in 1220. The Paris school together with the one in Oxford became the intellectual centers of the West.[21] Saint Thomas attended the school in Paris.

The intellectual battle of the high Middle Ages was in two camps. One school of thought was led by Saint Bernard of Clairvaux (Franciscans). Bernard said you could find more in forests than in books, although he praised poetry. He represented the distrust of science and reason. He tried to bring Peter Abelard, the intellectual leader of the other camp (the Dominicans & Scholasticism), to trial for heresy. Eventually, the camp of reason won the day and the writings of St. Thomas Aquinas were widely accepted. Scholasticism is essentially the application of reason to revelation. It accepts the words of Scripture without question, but clarifies them by reason. Aquinas was a modern realist. Reason was God's gift to mankind and must

[20] Norman Kotker editor, Morris Bishop author, Middle Ages, American Heritage Pub. Co. Inc. 1968, page 131.
[21] Ibid., page 154.

necessarily confirm the truths of the faith. If it does not, than something has gone astray.[22]

Saint Thomas Aquinas was not without his critics: *"Scholasticism put an end to the confusion of philosophy with poetry, rhetoric, proverbial lore, and the various learning of the schools. The old connection between artes and philosophy is severed at a blow."[23]* So writes Ernst Curtius as he reflects on the decline of poetry and literature under the Scholastics, particularly under the writings of St. Thomas Aquinas. Other writers, like Brewer, are very critical of the Scholasticism, because it was far too pragmatic and rational. He calls St. Thomas Aquinas a "boy" who knows nothing of the world. Even major literary collections such as The World in Literature will acknowledge the impact of St. Thomas Aquinas on reason and attitudes of the high Middle Ages, but do not consider his works to be literary classics.[24]

FOURTH CLUE: THE FIRST ACCOUNTING BOOK WAS NAMED PROPORTIONALITY:

The first to promulgate generally accepted accounting principles (GAAP) was Pacioli.[25] His book

[22] Norman Kotker editor, Morris Bishop author, Middle Ages, American Heritage Pub. Co. Inc. 1968, page 274.

[23] Ernst Robert Curtius, translated by Willard Trask, European Literature and the Latin Middle Ages, published by Harper & Row N.Y. 1953, page 213.

[24] Robert Warnock and George Anderson, The World in Literature, published by Scott, Foresman and Co. two vol. The Ancient Foundations & Centuries of Transition, 1967.

[25] There is considerable dispute over the name Pacioli as it was translated. Some scholars prefer Paciolo. The name used for some of the later books was Fra. Paciolo di Borgo Santo Sepolcro. In certain books his name is Patiolus.

was titled <u>Summa de Arithmethica, Geometria, Proportioni et Proportionality,</u> and was first published in 1494, about two hundred years after the earliest record of double entry accounting.[26] Pacioli does not claim to have invented the system, and does not give any indication of the original author other than it is the method of Venice (chapter one). The writings of Pacioli are full of references to scripture and to the providence of God. He says that every journal page is to have the name of God (Sweet Jesus) at the top or at a minimum the cross of Christ. According to Pacioli, the use of God's name on every page is a generally accepted accounting principle. Near the end of the book, in chapter 34, he asks the readers to "pray to God for me that I may proceed by always doing well to His praise and glory." When he mentions the closing of the profit and loss account, he says, *"If the loss exceeds the profit, may God protect each of us who is really a good Christian from such a state of affairs, then credit the account in the usual manner."* Making a profit is good, in the beginning of his book he says: *"The end or objective of every businessman is to make a lawful and satisfactory profit so that he may remain in business."* [27]

Three issues can be observed from the first author of accounting: #1 the term proportionate was the title

[26] John Geijsbeck, <u>Ancient Double-Entry Bookkeeping,</u> Scholars Book Co. Houston Texas, 1914. The best collections of the works of Paciloli are at the Geijsbeck-Lawrence Library in Denver and at Harvard University Library, Cambridge, Mass. The second printing of the Summa was in 1523.

[27] There are two translations of the Summa into English. The most accurate was by Pietro Crivelli, but the most readable was by John B. Geijsbeek. Most scholars prefer the translation by Geijsbeek as illustrated above.

given to the section on accounting. #2 the accounting system was directly linked to the spiritual writings of the clergy. #3 Pacioli does not claim to have invented the double entry system. If Saint Thomas was the major influence on the development of double-entry accounting, then the references to the providence's of God and the concern for a just profit are entirely appropriate. If, on the other hand, the first accounting system did not develop within the clergy then the scriptural references that were considered the standards of the time, seem strangely misplaced just as they would today. The significance of the endorsement to permit the making of a profit by merchants, first argued by Saint Thomas Aquinas, should not be underestimated. His motive for influencing the development of an accounting system would be the control of a "just profit." The same theme was woven into the writings of Pacioli as he tried to promulgate this spiritually integrated accounting system.

The use of the label **proportionate** is a significant clue. The Greek word from which we get the English word proportionate is "analogos".[28] An analogy is the correspondence between things otherwise dissimilar.[29] What is a journal entry but an analogy? The early authors of accounting perceived the journal entry as the critical part of the system, the book of original entry. Pacioli went into great detail to illustrate each

[28] Walter Bauer's, <u>Arndt and Gingrich, Greek-English Lexicon of the New Testament and Other Early Christian Literature,</u> University of Chicago Press, 1877-1960, page 57, "right relationship, proportion... in right relationship to..in agreement with..or in proportion to..."

[29] <u>The American Heritage Dictionary</u>, second college edition, Houghton Mifflin Co. Boston, page 106.

type of journal entry using double lines to separate the
"per" and the "a." (He preferred these to debits and
credits). How does the use of analogy connect with
Saint Thomas Aquinas? Scholars of his work refer to
him as the father of the analogy. Many scholars say
that this is what he is best known for.[30] The last point
deserves a note of caution. The analogy, for which
Saint Thomas Aquinas was famous, was a "logical
doctrine about the meaning of words."[31] He would not
have used the equal sign in his construction of an
analogy. They also did not use negative number during
this time period, hence the need for debits and credits.
Saint Thomas Aquinas loved to connect things together
in a conservation relationship.

Aristotelian theory of cause and effect was applied
to everyday life and to the nature of God by Saint
Thomas Aquinas.[32] What is a journal entry but the
recording of everyday events with a cause and effect? Is
it a powerful argument for connectivity that the life of
the person who advanced the theory of the analogy and
logic coincides exactly with the development of double-
entry accounting? As one scholar has noted, it was
actually the disciples of Saint Thomas Aquinas that

[30] David B. Burrell, Aquinas, University of Notre Dame Press,
1979, page 55. David Burrell tries to argue that
historians have taken the grammatical astuteness of
Aquinas as a replacement for his intuition. This is
interesting to David Burrell because he says "it
should direct us to his practice instead of to his
theory". Double-entry accounting may have been one
of the practices of St. Thomas Aquinas.

[31] Therese Bonin, a well published scholar on St. Thomas
Aquinas, commenting on this chapter and the theory
that Saint Thomas Aquinas used algebraic logic.

[32] Anthony Kenny, The Five Ways of St. Thomas Aquinas'
Proofs of God's Existence, University of Notre Dame
Press, 1969. (An excellent book on the formulations of
St. Thomas Aquinas).

turned his theory into methods (methods such as "proportioni et Proportionalita"):*"The philosophical activity of the master became doctrine in the hands of his disciples. Constructing a theory turned analogy into method and gave the discussion a particular turn: does it work?"*[33]

The invention of movable metal type in 1454 should also not be underestimated.[34] If Saint Thomas Aquinas or his disciples did in fact conceive the first double-entry accounting system that became known as the method of Venice, the printing press was not available to disseminate the information. When the press was available for use, other than for making Bibles, it was used by Pacioli. It is also interesting to note that subsequent accounting authors such as Manzoni said the same things as the <u>Summa</u> without giving credit to Pacioli.[35] This is further evidence that some lost manuscript by Saint Thomas Aquinas on Proportioni et Proportionalita was available to the early authors of books on mathematics.

FIFTH CLUE: LOCATION

The fifth clue can also be an argument against the hypothesis. St Thomas Aquinas was born in the family's castle at Roccasecca in central Italy. At the age of five he was placed by his parents in the monastery at Monte Cassino. He next enrolled at the University of Naples and then at the Dominican house of studies in

---

[33] David Burrell, <u>Aquinas,</u> U. of Notre Dame Press, 1979, page 55.

[34] This is the traditional date for the invention of printing from movable metal type. Usually attributed to Johann Gutenberg who lived from 1398 to 1468.

[35] There are about 50 books on accounting written between 1494 (Pacioli) and 1636 (the English book on the keeping of accounts "after the Italian manner").

Paris as well as spending some period of time in Rome. The first accounting book uses Venice as the reference point of origin. It does not appear that St. Thomas Aquinas ever lived in Venice the commercial capital of Italy or even passed that way in his travels. Naples and Rome are in the south and Venice is in the north. Cultural exchange between the two was limited. This is considered one of the major objections to the hypothesis that St. Thomas Aquinas or one of his disciples authored the first accounting book. The counter argument is that two hundred years passed between the work of St. Thomas Aquinas and the publication of the first accounting book. Did the Holy Roman Catholic church have the ability to influence the culture of Venice 730 miles away? The scholars who argue no to this question site the conflict between Rome and Venice during the 15th century. However, the conflict might explain why the first accounting book did not credit the author. If it did, it might be rejected as a work of the enemy. Can a great idea travel four miles a year (730/200)? After publication on the printing press it traveled to every country in the known world. It is great thing for accountants that the whole world uses the same system of debits and credits, thanks to the distribution by the Roman Catholic Church. Actually, only the Latin based languages use debits (debere in Latin) and credits, but the accounting theory is still the same from the United States to the China.

SIXTH CLUE: THE INFLUENCE OF THE HOLY SCRIPTURE AND THE NATURE OF GOD

What was the influence of the Holy Scriptures on the accounting equation? The Bible describes God as having a dual nature of justice and mercy. God's investment in creation was from his mercy. The Judean-Christian view of creation is that mankind committed an original sin and as a result "Justice" entered the relationship of Creation and Mercy. The Holy Scriptures teach that sin is a liability account and that the Justice of God demands that sin be satisfied. The lord's prayer for example in Matthew 6:12 uses debts for sin in both the King James and the NIV translations: "Forgive us our debts as we also have forgiven our debtors." In the explanation that follows (v. 14) Jesus uses "trespasses" in the King James and the word "sin" in the NIV when He explains the prayer. Forgiveness in the Old Testament was centered on the Sabbath Year as recorded in Leviticus chapter 25. The year of Jubilee was a time of forgiveness and liberty throughout the land. It was intended by God to be a fresh start for everyone. All debt was cancelled and the land was to return to the original owners. There is no historical record to indicate that the practice of Jubilee was ever followed, but God made total forgiveness available to us to day in the person of Jesus Christ. Jesus is the personification of the year of Jubilee. (Luke 4:21) Now that is GOOD NEWS!

"The spirit of the Lord is on me, because he has anointed me to preach good news to the poor. He has sent me to proclaim freedom for the prisoners and recovery of sight for the blind, to release the oppressed, and to proclaim the year of the Lord's favor."

God's accounting equation, after the fall of mankind, was His works, the assets of heaven and earth equal both the Mercy and Justice of God. (Heaven and Earth = Mercy + Justice) Sections of the writings of St Thomas Aquinas attempted to answer the question "Whether in every work of God there are mercy and justice?" His conclusion was yes, in every work of God, in all of creation there is both mercy and justice.[36] This profound relationship as taught by St. Thomas Aquinas was the inspiration for the modern accounting equation. Assets = Debt + Investment by the owner. Not that St. Thomas Aquinas would have used an equal sign in the relationship. Accounting has always been more about the truth in relationships than mathematics. Accounting is the process of recording objects and ideas in a proper and proportionate relationship. Proportionality was the forte of St. Thomas Aquinas.

FINAL COMMENTS:

The dominant theory on the origin of double-entry accounting is that it is "neither a discovery of science nor the inspiration of a happy moment, but the outcome of continued efforts to meet the changing necessities of trade."[37] The method of Venice is attributed to the merchants and bankers of Florence, Venice and Genoa during the thirteenth century.[38] Could a system such as double entry evolve over time? Possibly, but it has not evolved dramatically in the last 500 years. The text written by Pacioli could still be used in principles of accounting classroom today. Did it take the brilliance of a person such as Saint Thomas Aquinas to provide the missing ingredients of self-balancing accounts?

[36] *The Summa Theologica of St. Thomas Aquinas,* Second and Revised Edition, 1920 Literally translated by Fathers of the English Dominican Province, Online Edition Copyright © 2003 by Kevin Knight, http://www.newadvent.org/summa/102104.htm
[37] Richard Brown, ed. A History of Accounting and Accountants, Augustus M. Kelly Publishing, N.Y. 1968, page 93.
[38] Ibid. page 99.

The life of the father of the analogy living and teaching at the same time that proportionality was considered a part of the study of mathematics and bookkeeping is difficult to accept as coincidence. Note that Saint Thomas Aquinas was a practical and technical writer, not a poet or literature great. He was an Italian monk with an intense concern for a just price, which gave him every reason to address the accounting issue; his writings are full of economic issues. Would the merchants of Venice have integrated spiritual principles into the accounting system? It seems highly unlikely.

Saint Thomas Aquinas was the dominant intellectual figure of that time period, and the purpose and intent of his work coincides perfectly with the development of double-entry accounting. The rationale for the connection between the two is obvious. Perhaps, someday a manuscript will be discovered to prove or disprove this hypothesis. Until then, it makes a great topic for discussion and further research.

Bibliography

Abacus, December 1973

Aquinas, Thomas. Summa Theological.

Bauers, Walter. Arndt and Gingrich, Greek-English Lexicon of the New Testament and Other Early Christian Literature. University of Chicago Press, 1877-1960.

Brown, Richard ed. A History of Accounting and Accountants. Augustus M. Kelly Publishing, N.Y. 1968.

Burrell, David. Aquinas. U. of Notre Dame Press, 1979.

Curtius, Ernst Robert. Translated by Willard Trask.

European Literature and the Latin Middle Ages. Harper & Row, N.Y. 1953.

Geijsbeck, John. Ancient Double Entry Bookkeeping. Scholars Books Co. Houston, Texas, 1914.

Giddens, Anthony. Introduction to *"The Protestant Ethic and the Spirit of Capitalism by Max Weber"* Charles Scribner's Sons, New York, 1958.

Journal of Accounting Research. Spring 1973.

Kenny, Anthony. The Five Ways of St. Thomas Aquinas' Proofs of God's Existence. University of Notre Dame Press, 1969.

Kotker, Norman. Editor. Morris Bishop author. Middle Ages. American Heritage Pub. Co. Inc., 1968.

Landreth, Harry & Colander, David. History of Economic Thought. Houghton Mifflin Company, Princeton, N.J., 1994.

Langer, William. Editor. An Encyclopedia of World History. 4th. Edition, Houghton Mifflin Company, Boston, 1968.

Lee, Geoffrey A. *Abacus*. December, 1979.

Lee, Geoffrey A. The coming of age of double entry:

The Giovanni Farolfi Ledger of 1299-1300. The Accounting Historians Journal, Fall 1977.

Lee, Geoffrey A. The Florentine Bank Ledger Fragments of 1211, Journal of Accounting Research, Spring 1973.

Littleton, A.C. Accounting Evolution to 1900. U. of Alabama Press, The Academy of Accounting Historians, 1981.

Nottingham Medieval Studies, Vol XVI. 1972.

Pergallo, Edward. Origin and Evolution of Double Enty Bookkeeping, A Study of Italian Practice from the Fourteenth Century. American Institute Publishing Company, 1939.

The Roots of Writing. Time. August 1, 1977, page 76.

Warnock, Robert & Anderson, George. The World in Literature. Scott, Foresman and Co. Two Vols. The Ancient Foundations & Centuries of Transition. 1967.

Zaid, Omar Abdullah. *"The Accounting Historians Journal."* Vol. 27, No. 1, June 2000. by Birmingham Printing and Pub. Co. Al. 2000

PART III –
Supplemental
Lecture
Material

Chapter 5

ACCOUNTING IN THE GLOBAL VILLAGE

A SUMMARY OF INTERNATIONAL ACCOUNTING STANDARDS FROM A U.S. PERSPECTIVE

By
Dr. Jack E. Bower
Eastern University

We have become a global village. Respect for people from other backgrounds and empathy towards those of diverse faith and culture as become a basic professional competence in the 21st century. Competition for many industries is now defined globally. Trading in cross-boarder financial markets has become commonplace and discipline of accounting is rapidly becoming globally conceptualized. *"Love your neighbor as your self"* is a universal principle.

International trade and competition has achieved significant progress in the economic development of third world nations. Overall the standard of living continues to rise worldwide as a result of international trade as well as many positive changes in international policy environment. Financial information is the transmission element that makes trade possible. The role of international accounting standards in the global village is vital to this continuing success.

The International Accounting Standards Board (IASB) is an independent decision making body established in January 2001, similar in structure to the Financial Accounting Standards Board (FASB), which serves the same functions for the United States. The new structure was the recommendation of the "Strategy Working Party," established in 1997 by the International Accounting Standards Committee, the predecessor of the IASB.[1] The goal of the IASB is to promote uniformity in accounting principles around the world.[2] The United States has the world's largest economy and the most extensive and well-developed

[1] FASB description of the IASB "The new structure has characteristics similar to that of the FASB's structure. There is an IASC Board of Trustees, an independent, mostly full-time standard setting Board called the IASB, and an Advisory Council. The IASB held its first meeting to discuss technical issues in April 2001. Like the FASB, IASB meetings to discuss technical issues are open to the public." http://www.fasb.org/IASC/iasb.shtml

[2] IASB Constitution "The objectives of IASC are: (a) to develop, in the public interest, a single set of high quality, understandable and enforceable global accounting standards that require high quality, transparent and comparable information in financial statements and other financial reporting to help participants in the world's capital markets and other users make economic decisions; (b) to promote the use and rigorous application of those standards; and (c) to bring about convergence of national accounting standards and International Accounting Standards to high quality solutions." http://www.iasc.org.

collection of Generally Accepted Accounting Principles (GAAP). As of the summer of 2002, there are 145 FASB Statements of Financial Accounting Standards (SFAS), 7 Financial Accounting Concepts, 43 Interpretations and 97 Technical Bulletins. This significant collection of accounting literature continues to have a major impact on the development of IASB principles. Generally Accepted Accounting Principles in the United States and International Accounting Principles are very similar and continue to move towards mutual in most circumstatnes harmony.[3]

Here is an example of the standard setting process. On April 21, 1999 the FASB voted to rule out the Pooling of Interest Method of accounting for business combinations forcing the use of the purchases method, which creates goodwill. This was a significant move towards harmonization. The Wall Street business community in the U.S. complained about the FASB ruling to Congress, and after much debate, it was vetoed by the S.E.C. In the summer of 2001, the FASB issued SFAS 142, to no longer require the amortization (expensing) of goodwill created by the purchases method (the expensing of goodwill was lowering projected earnings from mergers). This removed the objection to the use of the purchases method by corporations wanting to merge. In the end, everyone got what they wanted and the U.S. is now very close to IAS 22 & 40 which requires fair value reporting.

[3] FASB description of the differences between U.S. GAAP and International Standards "The FASB's obligation to its domestic constituents demands that it attempt to narrow the range of difference between the U.S. and other countries' standards. High-quality financial information is essential to analysis and assessment of investment opportunities to ensure the efficient allocation of capital both within and across national borders." http://www.fasb.org/IASC/

However the decrease in the value of goodwill is an audit issue for public accountants to address each year. The point is that we are moving towards a more unified set of accounting standards! Are we there yet?[4] No, but in cases where they are not similar, the U.S. method is generally permitted. For example, the Last In First Out (LIFO) method of inventory valuation is U.S. GAAP and permitted by international standards. The other 103 countries that belong to the IASB almost universally reject it.

International Accounting Standards, when viewed from a U.S. perspective appear less complicated and less complex than U.S. GAAP. IASB principles are designed to provide the minimum amount of guidance. This also means that a significant amount of double accounting treatments are permissible. The IASB Board refers to the preferred method as a "benchmark" so as not to offend the country using the less preferred method.

---

[4] FASB view of the need for harmonization "Ideally, international analysts and investors would like to compare   financial statements (both domestic and foreign) based on the same accounting standards, especially if those standards raise the overall quality of financial information. At present, a single set of high-quality international accounting standards that is accepted in all capital markets does not exist. In the United States, for example,   domestic firms that are registrants with the Securities and Exchange Commission (SEC) must file financial reports using U.S. generally accepted accounting principles (GAAP). Foreign firms filing with the SEC can use U.S. GAAP, their home country GAAP, or international standards—although if they use their home country GAAP or international standards, foreign issuers must provide a reconciliation to U.S. GAAP." http://www.fasb.org/IASC/

For more information contact:
International Accounting Standards Board
30 Cannon Street, London EC4M 6XH,
United Kingdom
Telephone: +44 (0)20 7246 6410
Facsimile: +44 (0)20 7246 6411
Publications Facsimile: +44 (0)20 7353 0562
E-mail: iasb@iasb.org.uk

The following list and brief comparison provides a framework for discussion of International Accounting Standards and U.S. GAAP. Summary information is available over the web at: http://www.iasb.org/standards/summaries.asp http://www.fasb.org/st/

IAS 1 – PRESENTATION OF FINANCIAL STATEMENTS

The IAS 1 defines the overall considerations for the basic four financial statements; fair presentation, accounting policies, going concern, accrual basis of accounting, consistency, materiality and aggregation, offsetting and comparative information. The standard prescribes the minimum structure and content including certain information required on the face of the financial statements.

This is similar in coverage to the six Statements of Financial Accounting Concepts (SFAC) with some notable exceptions such as the lack of the requirement for the distinction of current/noncurrent assets in the Balance Sheet.

IAS 2 – INVENTORIES

Lower of cost (which include costs to bring the inventories to their present condition and location) or net realizable value. If cost cannot be determined, then

LIFO (with disclosure requirements) or weighted average formulas are permitted.

The permitting of the LIFO method is a concession to the U.S. Similar to L.C.M. in the U.S. FASB Statement No. 151, Inventory Costs—an amendment of ARB No. 43, Chapter 4 (Issue Date 11/04)

IAS 3 – CONSOLIDATED FINANCIAL STATEMENTS

The IAS 3 superseded by IAS 27 (1989) and IAS 28 (1989).

IAS 4 – DEPRECIATION ACCOUNTING

The IAS 4 superseded by IAS 16 with respect to depreciation of property, plant and equipment. Superseded by IAS 38, with respect to amortization of intangible assets. Withdrawn.

IAS 5 - INFORMATION TO BE DISCLOSED IN FINANCIAL STATEMENTS

The IAS 5 superseded by IAS 1.

IAS 6 - ACCOUNTING RESPONSES TO CHANGING PRICES

The IAS 6 superseded by IAS 15.

IAS 7 – CASH FLOW STATEMENTS

Cash flow statement is divided into operating, investing, and financial activities. Direct or Indirect method is permitted.

The same format as the U.S. FASB No. 95 (1987) but with more detail and disclosure in the footnotes.

IAS 8 – NET PROFIT OR LOSS FOR THE PERIOD, FUNDAMENTAL ERRORS AND CHANGES IN ACCOUNTING POLICIES

The IAS 8 separate disclosure in the notes is required for extraordinary items and ordinary but abnormal items of income and expense. Changes in accounting estimates are reflected prospectively. Correction of an error is treated as a prior period adjustment and a change in accounting policy is treated retrospectively by restating all prior periods presented.

This is similar to APB Opinion 9, 26, & 30 on extraordinary items and SFAS 4 on extinguishment of debt as extraordinary. Also see FASB Statement No. 154, **Accounting Changes and Error Corrections—a replacement of APB Opinion No. 20 and FASB Statement No. 3** *(Issue Date 05/05)*

IAS 9 – RESEARCH AND DEVELOPMENT COSTS

Superseded by IAS 38.

IAS 10 – EVENTS AFTER THE BALANCE SHEET DATE

The IAS 10 financial statements should be adjusted for events occurring after the Balance Sheet date that provide further evidence of conditions present before the Balance Sheet date. New information discovered before the issuance of the financial statements on conditions present before the Balance Sheet date should be disclosed in the financial statements. Financial statements should not be adjusted for events occurring after the Balance Sheet date that reflect on conditions occurring after the Balance Sheet date.

This is similar to US AICPA GAAS Section 560.03 to .09 but the IAS language is stronger.

IAS 11 – CONSTRUCTION CONTRACTS

The IAS 11 "Percentage of completion method" should be used if the contract price, past and future costs, and percentage of completion are known or can be reasonably estimated. If not, the "cost recovery method" should be used (costs are expensed and revenues are recognized to the extent of costs expensed). In both cases, expected losses should be recognized immediately. The "cost recovery method" varies from the "completed contract method" in that with the "completed contract method", no profits are recognized until the completion of the project.

This is similar to US GAAP (Accounting Research Bulletin 45, AICPA SOP 81-1, & APB 10).

IAS 12 – INCOME TAXES

The IAS 12 accrue for deferred tax liabilities for taxable temporary differences. Accrue for deferred tax assets for deductible temporary differences only if it is probable a tax benefit will be realized.

This is similar to SFAS 109 with a stronger emphasis on "reasonable expectation of realization" for the balance in the deferred taxes payable account.

IAS 13 – PRESENTATION OF CURRENT ASSETS AND CURRENT LIABILITIES

The IAS 13 superseded by IAS 1.

IAS 14 – SEGMENT REPORTING

The IAS 14 segment information by geographical area is required. If consolidated financial statements

are presented, the segment reporting is also consolidated. There are two bases for segmentation (primary and secondary), each with different disclosure requirements.
This is similar to SFAS 14.

IAS 15 – INFORMATION REFLECTING THE EFFECTS OF CHANGING PRICES

The IAS 15 is encouraged but not required unless required in the country of domicile. Current Cost Approach and Purchasing Power Approach are acceptable but there is no international consensus on the subject.

This was formerly a US requirement under SFAS 33, but was eliminated by SFAS 82.

IAS 16 – PROPERTY, PLANT AND EQUIPMENT

The IAS 16 initial measurement should be at cost, then depreciate. An alternative is to use the fair value approach. If the fair value approach is used, it should be used for all like assets. Unlike US GAAP, even under the depreciation cost method, revaluation is allowed.

Under US GAAP, the fair value approach is not allowed for Property, Plant and Equipment except as unaudited supplementary information.

IAS 17 – LEASES

The IAS 17 substance of the transaction over form of the contract. A finance lease (capital lease under US GAAP) is defined as one that transfers substantially all the risks and rewards to the lessee. A finance lease should be capitalized at the lower of fair value or the present value of lease payments. Operating leases are treated as current operating expenses. This is similar to SFAS 13.

IAS 18 – REVENUE
The IAS 18 is essential criterion for the recognition of revenue. This is similar to APB Opinion 10 & FAC 5.

IAS 19 – EMPLOYEE BENEFITS
The IAS 19 defined contribution plans are a trust account. Defined benefit plans require the use of actuarial principles.

A table is available on the IASC web site (www.iasc.org.uk) that illustrates the differences between IAS 19 and US GAAP.

IAS 20 – ACCOUNTING FOR GOVERNMENT GRANTS AND DISCLOSURE OF GOVERNMENT ASSISTANCE
"Grants should not be credited directly to equity, but recognized as income in a way matched with related costs. Grants related to assets should be deducted from the cost or treated as deferred income."

Deferred revenue is acceptable U.S. G.A.A.P., APB No. 29 & FASB EITF 86-29, but the recording grants as contra asset accounts are not.

IAS 21 – THE EFFECTS OF CHANGES IN FOREIGN EXCHANGE RATES
(Translation into one reporting entity, not between countries for the convenience of readers.) Transactions are recorded at the exchange rate on the transaction date. Differences between the recorded amount and the settlement amount are a gain or loss. Proper accruals should be made at year-end. Integral part of operations of the parent – effect of the exchange rate change has

an immediate impact on the monetary items held by the parent rather than just the parent's net investment in the operation (not an integral part). The translation of the foreign financial statements into those of the parent should achieve the same effect as if all transactions of the foreign operation had been entered into by the parent.

SFAS 52 recognizes the gain or loss between transaction date and settlement date. No standards for "integral part of operations." The IAS is more involved than the US standard.

IAS 22 – BUSINESS COMBINATIONS HAS BEEN REMOVED FROM THE LIST OF INTERNATIONAL ACCOUNTING STANDARDS.

The international community would prefer the Purchase Method to be used in most cases with the Pooling of Interests Method only to be used when nether party is identified as the acquirer. Goodwill is defined as the difference between the purchase price and the fair value of the net assets. The example of harmonization of accounting standards in the open section regarding business combinations has caused a problem for the IASB. The failure to expense goodwill is not acceptable to the international community, but because it is U.S. GAAP some concession will need to be made. Stay tuned for a future IASB pronouncement.

U.S. GAAP is SFAS 141, which supersedes APB Opinion 16, it requires business combinations to be accounted for using the purchase method. The Pooling of Interest Method was removed from US GAAP to provide more international harmonization. In addition, SFAS 142, which supersedes APB Opinion 17, eliminates the amortization of goodwill and requires an annual test for impairment instead. This is very different than the IAS, which does not permit an enterprise to assign an infinite life to goodwill and still requires the amortization method. The IAS requires annual testing for impairment, when the useful life of the goodwill is estimated to be more than 20 years.

IAS 23 – BORROWING COSTS

Capitalization of borrowing costs is not required. These requirements are "set out" if the enterprise elects to follow the capitalization approach.

This follows the US standard of SFAS 34 including the "not to exceed actual" requirement. US standard is more complex and specific.

IAS 24 – RELATED PARTY DISCLOSURES

The IAS 24 is similar in standards to the SFAS 57.

IAS 25 – ACCOUNTING FOR INVESTMENTS

The IAS 25 is superseded by IAS 39 and IAS 40.

IAS 26 – ACCOUNTING AND REPORTING BY RETIREMENT BENEFIT PLANS

This standard complements IAS 19. Applicable to insurance companies and any separate legal entity that is a trust for pension benefits. It simply defines the report contents for retirement benefit plans.

This is similar to AICPA Industry audit guides for the insurance industry. In the US, these types of organizations are a special type of nonprofit corporation. See FASB Statement No. 132 (revised 2003), Employers' Disclosures about Pensions and Other Postretirement Benefits—an amendment of FASB Statements No. 87, 88, and 106, (Issue Date 12/03)

IAS 27 – Consolidated Financial Statements and Accounting for Investments in Subsidiaries

The standard provides the framework for intercompany eliminations (intragroup eliminations). The word "subsidiary" is defined as an investment, where the power of control is exercised, but not necessarily over 50% control. If the investment "subsidiary" is covered under IAS 39 and IAS 40, then it is an investment and not part of the consolidated financial statements. Also, subsidiaries that are accounted for by the equity method under IAS 28 are not part of the consolidated financial statements.

Similar to U.S. FASB No. 115. The permitting of the equity method here and in IAS 28 is another concession to the U.S. The equity method is unique to the U.S. and considered illogical to most international accounting bodies.

IAS 28 – Accounting for Investments in Associates

Associate is defined as an enterprise in which the investor has significant influence. Both the Cost and Equity Method are permitted. Guidance is given as to which method would be appropriate. This is similar to U.S. GAAP

IAS 29 – Financial Reporting in Hyperinflationary Economies

Balance Sheet amounts not already expressed as in terms of the monetary unit current at the Balance Sheet date are restated by applying a general price index. If a general price index is not available, use the movement in exchange rate between the reporting currency and a relatively stable foreign currency.

Never exceed the recoverable amount (market value) of any restated items. Do not use IAS 21 when restating Balance Sheet accounts. Differences are credited to the "revaluation surplus" account. All movements are to be disclosed under IAS 5 including the basis for the restatement. Income statement amounts should also be restated by applying a general price index. Corresponding figures for previous reporting periods and consolidated financial statements are to be restated using the general price index approach.

Not fully a part of US GAAP or GAAS but the U.S. is moving in that direction. SFAS 107 Disclosure about Fair Value of Financial Instruments and the host of pronouncements on impairment such as SFAS 118, 121 & 137. SFAS 142, Goodwill and Other Intangibles also moved the U.S. closer to fair value accounting.

IAS 30 – Disclosures in the Financial Statements of Banks and Similar Financial Institutions

(See AICPA "Audit Guide for Banks".) Harmonization of the different methods of bank reporting and measurement or items in the financial statements is beyond the scope of this statement. This statement is simply a list of disclosures necessary for compliance with IAS.

IAS 31 – Financial Reporting of Interests in Joint Ventures

Jointly controlled operations – separate accounting records for the joint venture are not required.

Jointly controlled assets – separate accounting records are not required but if presented must be limited to the expenses incurred in common by the ventures and ultimately borne by the venturers according to their agreed shares.

Jointly controlled entities – application of "proportionate consolidation" only the venturer's share of the joint venture is reported in the consolidated financial statements. Separate financial statements are prepared in order to meet a variety of needs with the result that different reporting practices are in use in different countries. This statement does not indicate a preface for any particular treatment.

This is similar to US GAAP; Proportionate Share Accounting, APB Opinion 18 (Joint Venture = Partnership).

IAS 32 – FINANCIAL INSTRUMENTS: DISCLOSURE AND PRESENTATION

The IAS32 classification reflects substance, not form. What is debt - mandatorily redeemable preferred stock is debt and deduction of interest on the income statement. IAS 39 requires certain disclosures.

This is similar to SFAS 129 and SEC Accounting Rules, sec. 211.01 & 211.04. Note; substance over form is basic US business law

IAS 33 – EARNINGS PER SHARE

The IAS 33 is for public companies only, who must disclose basic and diluted net income on the face of the statement, and for each class of stock.

This is similar to APB Opinion 15 and SFAS 128 on Earnings Per Share.

IAS 34 – INTERIM FINANCIAL REPORTING

The IAS 34 contains both presentation and measurement guidance, defines the minimum content of an interim report, and sets out the accounting recognition and measurement principles to be followed in any interim financial statement.

This is similar to APB Opinion 28, which was clarified by SFAS 131.

IAS 35 – DISCONTINUING OPERATIONS HAS BEEN DISCONTINUED AS A STATEMENT.

It did not establish any new principles for deciding when and how to recognize and measure income, expense, cash flows and charges in assets and liabilities relating to a discontinued operation so it was removed.

This is similar to APB Opinion 30 as explained by the 1973 AICPA report, "Reporting the Results of Operations."

IAS 36 – IMPAIRMENT OF ASSETS

The IAS 36 deals with accounting for impairment of goodwill, intangible assets and property, plant and equipment. The standard includes requirements for identifying an impaired asset, measuring its recoverable amount, recognizing or reversing any resulting impairment loss, and disclosing information on impairment losses or reversals of impairment losses.

This is similar to SFAS 121. IAS 36 and SFAS 121 both use present value calculations to find the value of the asset.

IAS 37 – PROVISIONS, CONTINGENT LIABILITIES AND CONTINGENT ASSETS

The IAS 37 provisions should be recognized in the Balance Sheet when an enterprise has a present obligation as a result of a past event. The Statement uses the terms "probable" and "remote" as determining factors.

This is similar to SFAS 5 and Interpretation 34, but this IAS does not address obligations that are callable by the creditor, SFAS 78.

IAS 38 – INTANGIBLE ASSETS

The IAS 38 applies to advertising, training, start-up and R&D costs.

This is similar to SFAS 2, which states that enterprises must disclose all R&D expenses and APB Opinion 17, which states that enterprises must disclose the method of amortization. Under IAS, the items acquired for a particular research project that have no alternative future uses are expensed as items are used in the project. In contrast, such costs are expensed when incurred under GAAP in the US, Germany, and Mexico. Capitalization of R&D expenses occurs in Brazil and Japan. In Canada and the United Kingdom, the research costs are expensed and the development costs are capitalized.

IAS 39 – FINANCIAL INSTRUMENTS: RECOGNITION AND MEASUREMENT

Subsequent to initial recognition, all financial assets are remeasured to fair value, except those not held for trading or not held to maturity or whose fair value can not be readily measured.

This is similar to SFAS 115 and SFAS 133. The fair value of the hedge and accounting for the hedge depends on the type of hedge. A table comparing the IAS and US GAAP is available at the IASC web site (www.iasc.org.uk). See FASB Statement No. 149, Amendment of Statement 133 on Derivative Instruments and Hedging Activities, (Issue Date 4/03)

IAS 40 – INVESTMENT PROPERTY

The IAS 40 is not limited to enterprises whose main activities are in this area. Investment property is property (land or a building - or part of a building - or both) held (by the owner or by the lessee under a finance lease) to earn rentals or for capital appreciation or both. Investment property does not include property held as inventory, property under construction, finance lease (capital lease under US GAAP), regenerative natural resources and mineral rights. Under IAS 40, an enterprise must choose either the fair value model (investment property should be measured at fair value and changes in fair value should be recognized in the income statement); or the cost model (investment property should be measured at depreciated cost less any accumulated impairment losses). An enterprise that chooses the cost model should disclose the fair value of its investment property. IAS 40 also requires consistency in applying the chosen method to all investment property and discourages a change from one model to the other.

The U.S. is not ready to move to complete fair value accounting. The U.S. is however making progress in this direction. SFAS 142 is a good example, requiring the annual evaluation of the fair value of goodwill. SFAS 107 also requires market value accounting for investments which is very close to the international standard.

IAS 41 – AGRICULTURE

The IAS 41 prescribes the accounting treatment, financial statement presentation and disclosures related to agricultural activity. Biological assets and agricultural produce harvested from the biological assets should be measured at their fair value less estimated point-of-sale costs, except where fair value cannot be measured reliably. After the point of harvest, IAS 2 (Inventories) should be applied. The standard allows for biological assets to be measured at cost less any accumulated depreciation and any accumulated impairment losses if fair value is not reliably measurable. Enterprise must disclose reasons for this valuation.

This is not similar to U.S. GAAP. However, SFAS 40 Financial Reporting and Changing Prices: Specialized Assets, addresses the same issues from a U.S. perspective.

INTERPRETATIONS & ASSOCIATED DOCUMENTS:

The IASB has spent a lot of time trying to explain their standards, similar to problems faced by the FASB. Their explanations are called "Interpretations of International Financial Reporting Standards." These and what they call "Associated Documents" are also available in full text from their web site.

Chapter 6

PAY CEASAR WHAT BELONGS TO CEASAR, NO MORE AND NO LESS[1]

ESSENTIALS OF TAX RESEARCH

By
Dr. Jack E. Bower
Eastern University

INTRODUCTION

Accountants should practice tax avoidance, not tax evasion. Paying government agencies the proper amount and no more, fulfills the teaching of our Lord Jesus Christ and allows for a proper amount to be committed to God's activities. Giving more to Caesar than what Caesar deserves means less is available for God's purposes. The Apostle Paul confirmed this perspective of obedience in his letter to the Romans, chapter 13.

---

[1] Matt 22:21 The New Jerusalem Bible, Doubleday, N.Y. 1966.

"Everyone is to obey the governing authorities, because there is no authority except from God and so whatever authorities exist have been appointed by God. So anyone who disobeys and authority is rebelling against God's ordinance; and rebels must expect to receive the condemnation they deserve. Magistrates bring fear not to those who do good, but to those who do evil. So if you want to live with no fear of authority, live honestly and you will have its approval; it is there to serve God for you and for your good. But if you do what is wrong, then you may well be afraid; because it is not for nothing that the symbol of authority is the sword; it is there to serve God too, as his avenger, to bring retribution to wrongdoers. You must be obedient therefore, not only because of this retribution, but also for conscience's sake. And this is why you should pay taxes; too, because the authorities are all serving God as his agents, even while they are busily occupied with that particular task. Pay to each one what is due to each; taxes to the one to whom tax is due, tolls to the one to whom tolls are due, respect to the one to who respect is due, honour to the one to who honour is due."[2]

Determining the proper amount due to the Internal Revenue Service (IRS) can be an extremely complex matter. The shear volume of Internal Revenue Code, Regulations, Tax Cases and IRS publications is overwhelming without proper guidance. The purpose of the chapter is to provide the **research essentials** necessary to navigate our complex federal tax environment so

[2] Romans 13 The New Jerusalem Bible, Doubleday, N.Y. 1966.

that we can be *trustworthy in handling worldly wealth*[3] This knowledge is critical for the accountants of Christian ministries desiring to have IRS nonprofit status. After reading this chapter you should be ready to begin a topical study on a manual or electronic system. Learning to do tax research can help you lower your client's taxes and also provide some intellectual satisfaction.

Tax research requires time, patience and the proper resource materials. Obviously, accountants who practice in the U.S. must have a working knowledge of the Internal Revenue Code (IRC) in order to be an effective tax practitioner. A storehouse of tax research material is available to U.S. accountants at public libraries, university libraries over the web and of course, many accountants develop their own rather extensive libraries. The most widely used source for tax research **books** in the U.S. is Commerce Clearing House (CCH), Inc., 4025 West Peterson Aye, Chicago, Illinois 60646. The U.S. government (IRS) also uses CCH for its copies of the Code. Much of the material presented in this chapter is public information from C.C.H. publications. Several law schools have the entire U.S. Code, including the IRC (title 26), on the Internet. Some individuals also maintain the IRC and other useful tax information on the Internet. Unfortunately, the IRS does not maintain the Code and Regulations on the Net. They are available, however, as a part of the Federal

---

[3] Luke 16:9-13 The New Jerusalem Bible, Doubleday, N.Y. 1966.

Register on the site of the National Archives & Record Administration:

http://www.archives.gov/federal register/index.html

UNDERSTANDING THE OUTLINE OF THE INTERNAL REVENUE CODE

The first task in doing tax research is to understand the organization of the Code and Regulations. The Code is organized in a series of headings and subheadings, which, on the surface, appear very complex. A sample of these headings is given on the next page, in descending order from a very broad heading to a very narrow, specific section:

INTERNAL REVENUE CODE

Subtitle A Income Taxes
 Chapter 1 Normal Taxes & Surtaxes
  Subchapter A Determination of Tax
  Liability Part I Tax on Individuals
   Subpart A Nonrefundable
   Personal Credits

   Section 1 to 9602
    Subsection (a)
     Paragraph(1)
      Subparagraph (A)
      Clause (i)

The dotted line would not actually appear in the Code headings, but it has been added here to make the following point. The entire series of headings which appear above the dotted line (Subtitle A: Income Taxes through Subpart A: Nonrefundable Personal Credits) can be ignored for most research purposes. This is because the headings called "Sections" (below the dotted line) are numbered independently and do not depend on the bradiersheadings above them. The first section of the Internal Revenue Code is Section 1, and the last is Section +9600. Thus the tax researcher need only locate the proper Section to read without referring to the Subtitle, Subchapter, or Subpart, which that Section belongs to.

Then the researcher must find the proper paragraph or clause in the Code, using the headings indicated below the dotted line. For example, what if the researcher wanted to locate Internal Revenue Code Section 6104(e)? They would need to use the Code and find the page, which contains the heading "Section 6104(e)" at the bottom left-hand corner. If they wanted to find IRC Sec. 6104(e)(l) (B)(ii), they would simply follow the subheadings on the page containing Section 6104(e) as one would follow the pattern of any ordinary outline. In this example, Sec. 6104(e)(l)(B)(ii) would be referred to as Section 6104, Subsection e, Paragraph 1, Subparagraph B, Clause ii.)

What if the researcher wanted to locate provisions of the Code allowing for, say, public inspection of a nonprofit organization's financial information; the code section that makes a financial service such as GuideStar possible, http://www.guidestar.org.[4] This is an example of topical research and it demands a little more effort than locating a Section citation as in the previous case. The researcher would open the Code to the outline in the front and look for the Subtitle covering tax-exempt activities (in this case, Subtitle F). Then the appropriate Section could be found in Subtitle F, based on the Sections' titles. Section 6104's

[4] Guide Star provides financial information on nonprofit organizations. The site also has a copy of the Form 990 available using *Acrobat Reader*, for most nonprofits.

title is PUBLICITY OF INFORMATION REQUIRED FROM CERTAIN EXEMPT ORGANIZATIONS AND CERTAIN TRUSTS. Subsection 6104(e) is entitled, "Public Inspection of Certain Annual Returns and Applications for Exemption." These titles serve as signposts guiding the researcher to the part of the Code that addresses their tax question. The Code follows a format somewhat more complex than the chapter and verse designations of the Holy Bible. Each Section of the Code is commonly referred to as a "cite" which is short for citation. When this dissertation refers to 501(c)(3), it means IRC section 501, Subsection c, Paragraph 3. This is a cite.

This is how the Code is organized, but what about the organization of the Internal Revenue Regulations? The Regulations follow a system of headings similar to the Code. Just place a "1" in front of the Code Section in use and you will know the proper Regulations to read. For example, the Regulations on organizations discussed in Code Section 501(c)(3) are found in Regulation Sec. 1.501(c)(3). However, that is as far as the similarity between the Code and Regulations goes. The Subsection numbers in the Code, for example, are not equivalent to Regulation citations. Apart from the Section headings, the Regulations are organized differently from the Code. Most of the time a researcher will need to browse the Regulation Section which addresses the tax question to find the proper Regulation.

THE MASTER TAX GUIDE

There is an abbreviated way to do tax research. A Master Tax Guide has been designed for the U.S. to assist researchers in locating tax research information quickly and easily. Both the IRC and the Master Tax

Guide have an identical topical index. The Master Tax Guide can be ordered from CCH. Most professional tax researchers know the IRC so well that they can go to the proper section without an index. But most beginning tax researchers prefer the index in the Master Tax Guide over the index in the IRC because it is more user-friendly. The topical index of the Master Tax Guide gives a brief description of the law and regulations related to a researcher's question, helping him or her find the proper Code section or Regulation. The Master Tax Guide also gives information on court cases pertaining to various tax questions.

The Commerce Clearing House (CCH) version of the Master Tax Guide will also refer researchers to another type of tax publication, the CCH Standard Federal Tax Reports. These Federal Tax Reports discuss specific tax questions in detail, such as pension and employee benefits, automobile deductions or state taxes. The tax reports are produced by tax services such as CCH and are marketed to CPA firms and law firms in the U.S. to assist them in doing tax research. There are many tax services (other than CCH) offering such publications. Most research experts agree that the Bureau of National Affairs (BNA) is the most comprehensive of the tax services.

The Research Institute of America (RIA) is a newcomer to the tax research area and will not be found in the list of tax service providers in most law libraries. Most attorneys prefer BNA and it often includes sample forms for the legal profession to use. RIA is very popular with CPA firms. Either of these services, as well as CCH, can be helpful to the practicing accountant.

TAX SERVICES

Here is a list of the major tax services and the titles of their respective tax report publications:

Bureau of National Affairs(BNA)
Tax Management Portfolios

Commerce Clearing House(CCH)
Standard Federal Tax Reporter
Tax Treaties
Federal Estate & Gift Tax Reports

Prentice-Hall (PH) Thomson Publishing
Federal Taxes
Federal Taxes—Estate & Gift Taxes
Tax—Exempt Organizations

Research Institute of America (RIA) Thomson Publishing
Federal Tax Coordinator 2d

The practicing accountant will usually find the Code and Regulations to be of sufficient detail to meet his or her needs. However, the Regulations are written with a particular bias (the collection of tax), which the tax services will help the researcher to see through or around. This insight into ways of using the regulations to the researcher's advantage is referred to as "tax planning." Tax planning is what accountants and attorneys charge significant fees to perform.

LEGAL PRECEDENT – COURT DECISIONS ARE JUST AS BINDING AS THE CODE

If what has been explained so far were the whole story, tax research would be simple. The researcher would only need the books and services mentioned above. Unfortunately, the real world is an imperfect place, and U.S. Congressmen are imperfect persons. (This is no surprise to voters). When the U.S. Congress makes the tax laws, it does not always anticipate all the ways in which those laws will be applied, interpreted and scrutinized for loopholes. Who gets to settle the disputes over the interpretation of the Code and Regulations? The court system, of course, is the mechanism for resolving disputes between taxpayers and the Internal Revenue Service (IRS). Interestingly, the IRS is almost always the defendant in tax cases. The IRS does not need the court system to impound a checking account or place a lien against a taxpayer's property. The taxpayer, however, does need the court system to get relief from the strong arm of the IRS.

If an individual or organization pays a tax and then files for a refund, which the IRS refuses to pay, the taxpayer may have to request a trial. In this situation, the case would go to a District Court. If, on the other hand, the taxpayer <u>does</u> <u>not</u> pay the tax and desires to defend his or her action, the taxpayer must take the case to litigation. This may lead to a trial in Tax Court. Tax Court cases are legal proceedings before a single judge who will also review the case with other justices. Tax Court cases are not jury trials. Some of the best tax experts in the nation sit as justices on the Tax Court.

Most tax cases are disputes over interpretation of the law. The Tax Court has the authority to rule on several cases at once by deciding a particular case, which is similar to others. Unlike Tax Court rulings, rulings by a District Court are only binding within that court's judicial district and they have no impact on decisions in other districts. At the time a tax dispute goes to Tax Court, another individual or organization at an earlier point in time may have faced the same tax question. If the same issue has been litigated already, then the results of the earlier case might be ruled as binding on the case that is currently before the court. The court must follow legal precedent. Tax research through the study of court cases requires the use of parallelism.

Court decisions play a major role in determining how tax laws are to be carried out. Congress does not go back and revise the Code for each omission that it makes in tax law (and only on very rare occasions does it codify a court case). Instead, Congress is quite content to let the court system work out the finer details of how the law is applied. After all, Congress does not want to handle the often-heated political issues that come up as the law goes into effect. It is for the courts to straighten out the problems created by Congress. Thus court justices, in deciding a case, will go back to Congressional records to search for the intent of Congress in making the law. This is a difficult process and explains in part the current backlog of cases faced by the court system.

A typical example of the search for congressional intent in a tax case is that of a taxpayer challenging an IRS regulation. The issue before the court is whether or not the regulation at hand went beyond the scope of Congress' intention at the time it was put into effect by the Treasury Department. Many times tax researchers must also resolve a tax question by searching for the intent of Congress. This can be done by studying the Congressional Records, which recount the steps taken by Congress in enacting a law. These steps can provide clues as to Congress' intent in making a law.

U.S. taxpayers should view the Tax Court as the protector of their rights as U.S. citizens. Tax Courts are designed to give each tax case a fair and thorough review in order to render a just verdict.

RESEARCH OF CASE LAW

Most of the tax services mentioned earlier refer readers to selected court cases on critical tax questions, and give an overview of the results of each case. But what if the tax service doesn't provide any court cases on the topic being researched? How does the researcher find appropriate case material? Most of the time, tax researchers who are interested in any topic in general can find the court cases they need in what is called a "citator." This' is a separate published document which indexes court cases according to the tax questions they address. The best and most popular of the court case citators is called "Shepard's Federal Tax Citations." The major tax services also publish their own citators. Unfortunately, using a citator can be extremely tedious. For years, most tax researchers thought there had to be a better way.

Thankfully, there is a better way! That better way is to use an electronic data base service. All of the transcripts of every tax case in the U.S. have been entered into full—text computer software that can do a word search and locate specific court cases in a matter of seconds. These electronic libraries can provide a complete listing of all the court cases and journal articles on virtually any tax question. The volume of information these database services provide can be overwhelming. Individuals or organizations can purchase time on one of these legal databases using their own computers and a modem or broadband connection. Many CPA firms and law firms purchase time from these services regularly. The most popular is "Checkpoint" launched in June of 2002, it is operated by RIA.

ELECTRONIC DATABASE SERVICES

All of the major tax services offer web-based tax research. Lexis-Nexis is still considered the premier service, but it is also the most expensive. Many college, university, and public libraries subscribe to Lexis-Nexis and allow outside web access to their site. This means it is possible to find free web access, through a library site, to the most powerful tax database available over the web. Simply search the web for Lexis-Nexis Academic Universe and library sites will be available to you. Smaller libraries only permit access to Lexis-Nexis if you are on campus or protect the web access with passwords.

The most popular site to accountants is RIA (Research Institute of America) and their research database called "checkpoint." One nice feature about RIA is the upfront pricing, special offers, and a 30 day free trial http://www.riag.com/. They also aggressively market to academic institutions, offering free service to students for one semester as a means of their becoming familiar with RIA products.

Popular among legal professionals is West Publishing, which offers "WestDoc" as a tax research database http://creditcard.westlaw.com/. The great thing about WestDoc is the billing. They charge per document after you complete a registration form and agree to the "WestDoc Subscriber Agreement." Also very popular among the legal profession is a site maintained by Tax Analysts. Their database is called "TaxBase" and can be found at http://www.tax.org/. They are very upfront about the pricing. Federal tax research is based on usage and you can add other services for a minimal fee. Tax Analysts also has a free trial offer.

As previously mentioned, the publishing backbone of the tax research world is CCH Incorporated. The online store for CCH is http://onlinestore.cch.com. Their list of tax research publications is extensive. Their online research product can be found at http://tax.cchgroup.com/taxresearchnetwork/main.asp. Unfortunately their pricing for tax research is not available over the web. You have to talk to a sales representative.

Most of the databases present the search options in terms of different books or a library of research volumes. Each book represents a set of materials that can be searched electronically. The Code and Regulations, for example, represents one of the books. The Master Tax Guide or a student's textbook represents another book to search. The key to any electronic search is the key words used in the search. Too many words in the search will create the possibility of missing the topic and too few words mean an excessive number of search results to read. Electronic tax research is an art form that takes practice. There is more advice about electronic searches in the section entitled Substantial Authority.

HARD COPY RESEARCH

Tax court cases are also stored in published reference volumes. You will find that the citations used to locate specific cases will direct you to these reference volumes for information. Each volume contains the full text of a range of court cases. Each volume is published by a court reporting service and carries the name of that service. Similarly, every court citation includes the name of a court reporting service in abbreviated form. The name of the court reporting service in a court citation will signal the tax court case volume for which to look. The electronic database searches will also reference the same citations.

Below are some examples of court citations and the court reporting services to which they refer:

Cite listing	Court Reporting Service
S. Ct.	Supreme Court Reporter
AFTR	American Federal Tax Reports
USTC	U.S. Tax Cases
L. Ed.	United States Supreme Court Reports, Lawyers's Edition
U.S.	United States Reports
F.	Federal Reported
F.Supp.	Federal Supplement
Ct.Cl.	U.S. Court of Claims
TCM	Tax Court Memorandum
B.T.A.	Board of Tax Appeals Reports

Each court reporting service uses the same cover on all of its court case volumes. For this reason, finding the proper series of volumes in a law library can be a challenge. But once the researcher locates the proper set of volumes with the librarian's help, one should have little trouble finding the particular volume and page number with the court case needed. If the researcher only wants to check the general issue involved in a court case, then it is helpful to look at the short syllabus, which (in almost all cases) precedes that case.

ADMINISTRATIVE MATERIALS

The Internal Revenue Code consists of tax laws issued by Congress. As such, the Code is a legislative document. However, the Internal Revenue Regulations published by the U.S. Department of the Treasury are an administrative document. In addition to the Regulations, the Treasury Department often issues "revenue rulings" (abbreviated Rev. Rul.) and "revenue procedures" (Rev. Proc.). These statements allow the Internal Revenue Service to communicate its position on specific tax questions to the public without having to issue new regulations. Often, the Rev.Rul. and Rev.Proc. may come as a result of questions by several taxpayers or as a result of court cases. They are published weekly in the Internal Revenue Bulletin. A summary of these weekly bulletins comes out every (quarter/year) in a document called the "Cumulative Bulletin." The tax services and court reporting services will often refer to the Cumulative Bulletin, allowing the researcher to find Rev.Rul. and Rev.Proc. related to their tax question.

One might be particularly interested in reading a Rev.Rul. and Rev.Proc. during a major tax court case. For example, if the IRS litigates a case and happens to loose the case, the IRS can announce nonacquiescence on the issue in the Rev.Ruling. This nonacquiescence means that if the IRS lost the case in one district, it will still litigate the issue in a different district. The IRS can loose in several court districts (or circuits) and still win the overall court battle by appealing its best case to a higher court. Sometimes the IRS or a taxpayer appeals all the way to the Supreme Court.

SUBSTANTIAL AUTHORITY

Now to review the sequence for doing tax research under the U.S. system. Start with the index in the Code, the Master Tax Guide, or any other tax service guide. If an electronic database is available, selecting the key words for the search is the critical issue. It is highly efficient in an electronic search to start with more key words than might be necessary, thereby limiting the search to a very specific set of documents. If the search does not yield a match of key words within the same paragraph, then the key words are reduced by the least important word and the search is initiated for the second time. Generally, it is recommended to begin a search with the Master Tax Guide or with a tax textbook, so that the first explanation is the most complete. Next, search and read the relevant Code Section and Regulations. If more detail is needed, search for court cases and /or Rev.Rul. / Rev.Proc. related to the tax issue in question.

Manual searching also involves the selection of key words from the index. Sometimes a novice researcher will use a manual index to perform a general survey of the topic being considered thereby establishing the key concepts (words) at issue and then begin the electronic database search.

Researchers in such a complex system may have trouble resisting the temptation to skip over the Code and Regulations in favor of the more readable tax service publications. This strategy is ill advised because not all tax research carries the same weight with the IRS when penalties are being assessed or when tax disputes are being resolved in court. To the court system a regulation carries the full authority of a legal brief. And to the IRS the Regulations carry the weight of law. Therefore, if the position taken by the taxpayer is based on the Regulations, the Code, or a reported court case, the taxpayer will be in a better position to avoid a penalty from the IRS. If the authority for the action comes from one of the tax services such as RIA, it will not be regarded as "substantial authority" and may result in a penalty. Those who teach tax research will generally assign a grade based on the quality or "substantial authority" documented by the student

The ONLY Sources, which give substantial authority, are:

> Legislative
> Administrative
> Judicial

Secondary Sources are the tax services or textbook descriptions. The IRS is not impressed with ideas, opinion, or tax planning tips found in these services. The taxpayer will be at his or her own risk if he or she fails to provide Code, regulation, or judicial decisions to defend a tax position.

Bibliography

Blacks Law Dictionary, by Henry Campbell Black M.A. West Publishing Co. St. Paul Minn. (This dictionary is to the legal profession what the Webster dictionary is to most office people — An absolute necessity!)

Federal' Tax Research. Guide to Materials and Techniques, 3rd. Ed. Gail Levin Richmond, Foundation Press, N.Y.

Legal Research in a Nutshell, Morris Cohen, West Publishing Co., St Paul, MINN.

The Legal Research Manual. A game plan for legal research and analysis, Wren,

Published by A-R Editions Inc., Madison, Wisconsin.

Prentice—Hall Federal Taxes, Englewood Cliffs, NJ 07632

Research Institute of America. Inc. 90 Fifth Avenue, N.Y. N.Y. 10011

Using American Law Books, Alfred J. Lewis, Kendall/Hunt Pub. Co. Dubuque, Iowa.

West's Law Finder. A research manual for lawyers, West Publishing Co. P.O.Box 64526, St. Paul, MINN. 55164—9979

Chapter 7

PUBLIC CHARITY OR PRIVATE FOUNDATION

WHAT DOES IT MEAN TO BE A 501(C)(3) ORGANIZATION?

By
Dr. Jack E. Bower
Eastern University

God has blessed the U.S.A. beyond imagination. Particularly well blessed is the nonprofit sector which now represents about 30% of the U.S. economy in large metropolitan cities. The most common type of nonprofit organizations are public charities, which includes the church and countless Christian ministries. The most critical functions in American society are performed by public charities ranging from medicine to education.

The most important functions of the church are also being performed by Christian ministries.

> *"I tell you the truth, whatever you did for one of the least of these brothers of mine, you did for me....... For I was hungry and you gave me nothing to drink. I was a stranger and you did not invite me in, I needed cloths and you did not clothe me, I was sick and in prison and you did not look after me."*

Many U.S. churches focus primarily on spiritual needs. Those concerned about this description of the judgement day will often organize themselves into public charities to meet **both** spiritual and physical needs. The poor and needy all around the world are being directly impacted by U.S. based development organizations as they seek to meet the needs of others.

Every Christian accountant concerned about ministry outside the church need to understand the fundamental tax concepts governing the qualifications necessary to obtain and maintain public charity status. The continuation of the Lords work through various ministries depends on continued public charity status. Unfortunately this topic is highly technical in nature. The formulas presented in this chapter are used by the U.S. Internal Revenue Service (IRS) to determine public charity status and are sometimes not fully understood even by those who practice accounting or law.

THE FAVORABLE TAX ENVIRONMENT
Estate taxation has fueled the U.S. nonprofit sector. From the Revenue Act of 1916 until the repeal

starting in 2002, wealthy families have had two choices. Give a significant portion of the estate, about 55%, to the federal government in taxes or form a private foundation to administer the wealth.[1] Most would choose to form a private foundation and then have their children benefit as trustees. Private foundations must give 5% of their assets to public charities or spend 5% themselves on charitable activities. Most choose to fund public charities by awarding grants. Hence a significant amount of funding is available to public charities who properly apply for it. However, the tax incentive to form a private foundation has now changed. In June of 2001 President Bush signed into law a 1.35 trillion dollar tax cut. Part of the tax reduction package was the phase-out of the estate tax over time with a total repeal by the year 2010. A coalition of nonprofit organizations is fighting the phase-out and repeal. Their website is http://www.ombwatch.org.

Tax laws also favor the giving of property to public charities. The amount of the donation (and deduction) is equal to the fair market value of the property regardless of the price paid for the property. Gifts of appreciated property avoid capital gains tax and provide a shield from paying income tax in the form of a charitable contribution deduction.

ONCE TAX EXEMPT ALWAYS TAX EXEMPT?

Many accountants and managers of nonprofit public charities assume that their "public charity" status is irrevocable, not realizing that every two years, the IRS reviews the records (on Form 990) submitted by each 501(c)(3) organization to determine whether or not it still qualifies as a public charity. If

[1] Paragraph 42, 1999 U.S. Master Tax Guide.

the organization no longer qualifies, the organization may be forced into the less desirable status of a "private foundation." The IRS can revoke exemption without a hearing.[2]

THE DIFFERENCE BETWEEN PUBLIC CHARITIES AND PRIVATE FOUNDATIONS

What is the difference between a public charity and a private foundation, and why is there a problem if an organization loses its status as a public charity and becomes a private foundation? All 501(c)(3) organizations are classified as either public charities or private foundations. The difference between these two types of 501(c)(3) organizations is almost as great as the difference between the government of the U.S. and China. Private foundations must give away a certain percentage of their assets each year. Penalties for noncompliance with this rule are severe and can be imposed on both the manager(s) and the organization itself. No such restriction exists for public charities.

Congress created these harsh restrictions for private foundations because it perceived that wealthy individuals were using private foundations as a front for amassing huge private fortunes tax-free. Critics have called the rules for private foundations "overkill." But whether the rules go too far or not, they can create such an administrative headache that any 501(c)(3) organization that does not intend to operate as a private foundation should therefore guard its public charity status at all costs.

The situation is further complicated by the fact that the IRS also has imposed strict requirements on 501(c)(3) organizations registered as public charities. If a public charity fails to comply with IRS requirements,

[2] Metzger Est.,100 TC No.14

it can be penalized by being turned into a private foundation automatically. This is considered a penalty precisely because of the heavy load of restrictions imposed on private foundations.

How easy is it for an organization to lose its public charity status? In some cases, very easy! The U.S. congress created a set of rules to make sure public charities have a broad base of public support. Basically, all a public charity has to do to get in trouble with the IRS is receive one or two very large gifts from an outside source. The IRS tries to make this point clear on its form 990 but, many accountants who complete these forms with detailed financial information about their organizations do not realize how the IRS intends to use it to determine their eligibility to remain a public charity.

WHAT CONSTITUTES A PUBLIC CHARITY?

Public charities and private foundations are defined in the Internal Revenue Code section 501(c)(3). There are many types of nonprofit organizations but only 501(c)(3) organizations can accept tax deductible charitable contributions. There are basically five tests necessary to become an exempt organization as defined in IRS regulation 1.509 & 1.501(c)(3)-1:

Organizational and operational tests. Commonly referred to as the purpose test. Does the organization have an exempt purpose? First there is the paper test. Do the Articles of Incorporation and Bylaws clearly state the charitable purpose? Next is the smell test. Does the organization really and truly operate for a charitable purpose? Are the activities limited to those described in section 501[c][3].

No private inurement. The word inurement means getting use to something over time. The IRS uses this word to refer to individuals becoming accustomed to receiving personal benefits from a nonprofit organization. It is also a Biblical concept. Over time, we can be seduced by sin into thinking that nothing is wrong. The point is that there can be no distribution of earning in any form to individuals or private shareholders.

No propaganda to influence legislation. The political activities of nonprofit organizations are extremely limited. There is a fine line between distribution of information on a topic and trying to influence legislation. Support for a particular candidate is a violation. Even holding a debate where preference is shown for or against a certain candidate is wrong. Violation will result in a revocation of exemption or an excise tax on the organization. If this is your organizations issue, consider filing an election on IRS Form 5768.

The assets must be dedicated for an exempt purpose. One of the critical tests will be the distribution of the assets on dissolution. It must be clearly stated in the articles of incorporation that the assets upon dissolution will go to another organization "to be used in such a manner as (in the judgment of the court) will best accomplish the general purpose for which (the dissolved organization was organized.)" [3]

Public support test to determine public charity or private foundation status. The eligibility criteria for organizations seeking public charity status are complex but extremely critical if applicants are to avoid private foundation status. Public charities must pass one of a set of "tests" designed by the IRS to make sure they have a broad support base. If they do not satisfy one of the tests,

---

[3] IRS Regulation 1.501(c)(3)-4.

then they are automatically a private foundation. In other words, they must seek qualification as a public charity and actively maintain that qualification. The tests are found in section 509(a) of the Internal Revenue Code. The reminder of this chapter will outline the four basic tests used by the IRS. The form used to apply for public charity status is the Form 1023 and must be done within 27 months of creation or date operations began. It is also necessary to first file Form SS-4 to obtain an identification number needed on the application. Form 2848 will allow your accountant or attorney to represent the organization in matters regarding the application. Form 8718 is necessary to remit the user fee and Form 872-C is necessary to provide consent to have public charity status reviewed after 5 years. Questions can be directed to the IRS at Exempt Organizations Customer Service: 1 877 829 5500.

THE TESTS OF IRC SECTION 509(A)

"For purposes of this title, the term private foundation means a domestic or foreign organization described in section 501(c)(3) other than [the following tests].."(Section 509).

An organization seeking public charity status must meet any one of the following tests. An organization is not required to pass more than one test to qualify. IRS Publication 557 – Tax Exempt Status for Your Organization should also be consulted.

Test #1 is entitled "Reason for Non-Private Foundation Status" and is found in section 509(a)(l). This test has two parts. **Part One** of the test names specific types of organizations that can qualify automatically as public charities simply by virtue of the type of organization they are. This part of the Code states that:

"Any organizations described in section 170(b)(l)(A) of the IRC other than in clauses (vii) and (viii)" are public charities. In other words, in order to be eligible to receive charitable contributions, an organization must be described in 170(b)(l)(A). (Section 170 is part of a long section of permissible tax deductions.)

Sec.170(b)(l)(A) of the Code includes a list of organizations as follows:

(i) a church or a convention or association of churches

(ii) an educational organization which normally maintains a regular faculty and curriculum and normally has a regularly enrolled body of pupils

(iii) an organization the principal purpose or functions of which are the providing of medical or hospital care or medical education or medical research

(iv) organizations which operate exclusively to serve state colleges. (This is a paraphrase of the law.) This section was created for the land grant state colleges.

(v) a governmental unit

(vi) an organization referred to in subsection 170(c)(2) which normally receives a substantial part of its support ... from a governmental unit ... or from direct or indirect contributions from the general public.

Test #1, part one, provides public charity status to four types of nonprofits. Churches, educational institutions, governmental agencies, and medical organizations which are exempt from tax by definition. Church organizations in these categories generally do not have to be concerned about losing their public charity status.

What about an organization which is not a part of the prior list of organizations that automatically qualifies? Those organizations, not listed above in (i) through (vi), must meet the conditions of subpart (vi) of Section 170.

Test #1, part two. The Internal Revenue Regulations use a specific formula to determine whether or not an organization is receiving a *"substantial part of its support"* from a broad public base. The formula is applied to nonprofits that are neither churches, schools, government agencies, nor medical organizations.

The formula, described in Regulation l.170A-9(e)(7), aims to determine that a minimum of one third of an organization's total financial support is from the general public. This test is commonly referred to as the "one-third" (or thirty-three and one— third percent) support test. In any organization, the ratio of public to total support must be thirty-three and one-third percent or more in order for the organization to qualify as a public charity. Congress wants to make sure that public charities are not being used by only a few large donors as a refuge from taxes. This public-support formula is Congress' plumb line.

SCHEDULE A, PART IV, BOX 11

The IRS builds this one-third support ratio (or fraction) using financial information provided to the IRS on Form 990, Schedule A, Part IV box 11 and Part IV-A, lines 26, a to f. The tax regulations specify what types of support an organization should include in this fraction when it is trying to determine whether it qualifies as a public charity. To qualify as a public charity, an organization should aim to include as much revenue in the numerator of the fraction as possible in order to achieve the required one-third percentage. The calculation from the data it provides on Form 990 is clearly defined as the public support percentage and the organization should know immediately if it has fallen below the one-third-support threshold. Note that the calculation is based on four, years of data because the IRS uses a four-year average of revenue to determine the fraction.

Here is a summary of the box 11 test, found on Part IV-A, lines 15 to 26, Schedule A Form 990:

IRC 509(a)(1)
IRC 170 (b)(1)(A)(vi)
IRS Regulations 1.70A-9(e)(7)
"More than 33 1/3 Support Test" on a 4-year moving total

SOURCE OF SUPPORT	NUMERATOR	DENOMINATOR
Gifts, Grants, Contributions:		
From Qualified Sources	include	include
All government grants (not contracts)	include	include
From all other 170(b)(1)(A) organizations	include	include
From Disqualified Sources (amount over 2% of Total Support over four years)	exclude	include
Membership Fees:		
To belong to the organization	include	include
To purchase a service or merchandise	exclude	include

ORGANIZATIONS THAT DEPEND PRIMARILY ON GROSS RECEIPTS OR GOVERNMENT CONTRACTS FOR THEIR FINANCIAL SUPPORT MUST USE THE 509 (a)(2) TEST.

SOURCE OF SUPPORT	NUMERATOR	DENOMINATOR
Gross Receipts from related activities:		
Sales of merchandise	exclude	exclude
Performance of a service	exclude	exclude
Furnishing of facilities	exclude	exclude
Admission fees	exclude	exclude
Gross Receipts from unrelated business activities	exclude	include
Government Contracts for public facilities such as		
Libraries, Nursing Homes, Child Care	include	include
(Significant research grants will force the use of the 509(a)(2) test.)		
Gross Investment Income	exclude	include
Contribution of services (Donated services)	exclude	exclude
Support from a feeder organization		
509(a)(3) organization	exclude	exclude
509(a)(3) organization	exclude	exclude

IF THE NUMERATOR, DIVIDED BY THE DOMINATOR is more than 33 1/3, the organization passes the public support test.

The regulations also provide for another test under 509(a)(l), 170(b)(l)(A)(vi). This test is commonly referred to as the facts and circumstances test under test #1. It is the test of last resort. This test is for organizations that fail all other tests for being a public charity under test #1 or test #2.

To be considered under the facts and circumstances test, an organization must have at least ten percent public support. Of course public support would be less than thirty-three and one-third. The result is that the IRS must make a judgment call. All the organization can do is present the facts in a manner favorable to the organization and pray for good results. The IRS is not adversarial in dealing with nonprofits regarding the support test. The revenue agent might even suggest some changes that will improve the case for public charity status. Here is a brief outline of test:

FACTS AND CIRCUMSTANCES TEST

Ten percent is the minimal requirement to be considered under the facts and circumstances rule.

If the 10% test is met, the next issue is actual and planned solicitation.

Is the organization organized and operated to attract public and government support on a continuing basis?

Is the scope of fund raising activities reasonable in light of activities?

Is it a lack of start-up funding keeping the organization from expanding their solicitation program?

Endowment – If from a few individuals – unfavorable If from the government or general public – favorable

Does the governing body represent the broad interest of the general public? Community leaders and public officials are viewed as representing the public interest.

Does the organization provide facilities or services directly for the benefit of the general public on a continual basis?

Does the general public participate in the organization's activities?

This is a brief overview of the test. Consult the regulations for a complete summary.

Test #2 is found in Code Section 509(a)(2). This test is another support test. Organizations can use Test #2 if they do not qualify as public charities under Test #1. Organizations which do not qualify by virtue of the type of organization they are, must qualify by how they are supported. An organization does not qualify as a public charity on the basis of what it does. This is a common misconception!

SCHEDULE A, PART IV, BOX 12

Like test #1, test #2 has two parts. The first part of Test #2 is commonly referred to as the "more than one-third support test." This is the same formula as that used under Test #1 with two differences. First, the formula used in Test #1 is called the "thirty three and one third" support test (meaning 33 1/3 percent), whereas the formula in Test #2, part 1 is called the "one third" support test. There is no difference here in terms of mathematics but only in terms of labeling.

The real difference is that organizations that depend PRIMARILY on income from fees for services they perform must use the 509(a)(2) formula. Thus, the Test #1 formula applies to organizations with only donated (i.e., not earned) income.

The second part of the second test sets a maximum limit rather than a minimum limit. In this part of test #2, the part of an organization's income that comes from unrelated business activities and investments cannot exceed one third of that organization's total support. If it does, the organization fails this test. Organizations can deduct business-related expenses from their business income in this calculation. Here is a summary of the second test as found on Schedule A, Part IV box 12 and Part IV-A lines 27, a to h:

IRC 509 (a)(2) TEST
More than one-third of support On a four-year moving average Regulation 1.509(a)-3

Source of Support	Numerator	Denominator
Gifts, Grants, Contributions:		
From Qualified Sources	include	include
All government grants (not contracts)	include	include
From all other 170(b)(1)(A) organizations	include	include
From Disqualified Sources (gives over $5000. in total from all years OR an amount over 1% of Total Support over four years) (Exclude larger of amount over $5000 or 1% from any one source)	exclude	include

Public Charity or Private Foundation

SOURCE OF SUPPORT	NUMERATOR	DENOMINATOR
Membership Fees:		
To support the organization	include	include
To purchase a service or merchandise *(Exclude larger of amounts over $5000 or 1% from any one source)*	include	include
Gross Receipts from related activities:		
Sales of merchandise	include	include
Performance of a service	include	include
Furnishing of facilities	include	include
Admission fees (Exclude larger of amounts over $5000 or 1% from any one source)	include	include
Gross Receipts from unrelated business activities Exceptions: Sales for the convenience of members Sales using all volunteer labor Selling of donated merchandise	exclude	include
Gross Investment Income (Interest, Royalties, Rents)	exclude	include
Capital gains on Sale of Property	exclude	exclude
Contribution of services (Donated services)	exclude	exclude

IF THE NUMERATOR, DIVIDED BY THE DOMINATOR is more than one-third, the organization passes the public support test.

Test #3 is found in section 509(a)(3) of the Code. Organizations that qualify under this test have a parent organization that is already a public charity. The supporting organization must exclusively serve the parent in order to qualify under this test.

Test #4 is a test for organizations which test for public safety and is found in 509(a)(4).

INTERRELATIONSHIP OF THE TESTS

The material at the end of this chapter presents a summary outline of the tests for public charity status. The concepts seem very simple but the application of these concepts can be very complex. Those who work in this area on a daily basis refer to public charity status as a "form of art" because there are many various shades of meaning associated with these Code sections and Regulations.

Which test has priority in the IRS' evaluation? Some organizations will qualify under more than one test. However, the IRS' determination letter will always use the 509(a)(l) test if the organization qualifies under more than one test. The organization selects the test it wants the IRS to use by checking the proper box on Form 990, Schedule A. Most will choose box 11 or 12 as outlined above. The significance of these boxes is not clear on the 990 Schedule A, but the instructions for Form 990 Schedule A are helpful. Following are some terms in the IRS Code and Regulations that are critical to an understanding of the public charity tests.

QUALIFIED SOURCE[4]

Not everyone who gives to a public charity is actually helping the organization. Large grant makers are very aware of the damage they can do to a public charity. If a grant from one source is too large, it can cause an organization to fail the 509(a) tests and lose its public charity status. Interestingly, in such a case, the IRS can impose severe penalties on the donor as well as the public charity. Thus, many foundation grants require matching funds from the public at large. The grant givers are not only interested in protecting the public charities that receive their grants; they are protecting themselves!

How does a public charity determine whether an incoming gift or grant is too large? The first issue to be addressed is "Substantial Contributor" as defined under 507(d)(2). If the donor is a substantial contributor, the gift will be considered as being from a disqualified source and therefore not counted in the public support portion of the fraction under the code for test #2.

A second group of disqualified donors are the "Disqualified Persons" as defined in 4946 (a). All major donors and board members must be reviewed against these two legislative standards for exclusion from public support under test #2. If the donor is excluded from public support, the entire amount of their gift is excluded. Therefore, organizations must be very careful which test they are using and under which standards they evaluate their donors.

Test #1, part 2 (the thirty-three and one third support test as defined in the regulations, not the code), states that no gift from any one source may exceed 2% of the organization's total support. Any

4 I.R.C. 4946(a)(2)

amount above the 2% threshold is excluded from the organization's public support base. In other words, part of the gift of a qualified source does not count towards public support if they exceed the 2% threshold. In test #2, part 1, the threshold for qualified sources is only one percent. Please note the 1% test is for qualified sources not disqualified sources.

Form 990, Schedule A asks for the calculation of the 2% and 1% thresholds that are used to determine who is qualified or not qualified as a public source on the Support Schedule, Part IV-A, lines 25 and 26. Another critical point regarding the 2% test is that it is based **on cumulative donations** over time. Form 990 stipulates that the organization add the contribution of each source over a four-year moving average. This adding of all the years' gifts for each contributor is what many organizations fail to do until audited.

In the test #2, the Schedule A threshold for individual sources is 1% of an organization's total revenue OR $5,000, whichever is larger. For example, if total revenue was $100,000, then the $5,000 would be the benchmark not 1% of $100,000 which is $1,000. If the gift was 6,000, then 5,000 of this gift would be included in the tally of public support. If the gift was 4,000, then the full $4,000 would be included in the public support base. If total revenue was $1,000,000 then $10,000 would be the benchmark for inclusion in the numerator of the support fraction (the public support measure).

Once a donor becomes disqualified, he or she remains disqualified until they pass the "good boy" test. The "good boy" test is found in IRC Section 507(d)(2)(C). If the disqualified contributor does not give anything to the public charity for the next ten years nor is involved in management of the organization, then that person can again become a qualified donor. The point Congress is making is very obvious; Congress does not want an individual person or organization to have control of public charities. The organization must be responsive to the general public rather than the private interests of one individual or family.

It is very important to note that unlike test #2, which excludes the entire gift of a disqualified donor, the 2% test of test #1 only excludes the amount over the 2%. This means that at least some of the gift is included in the numerator when calculating the 33 & 1/3 support test in test #1.

UNUSUAL GRANTS

Unusual grants can be excluded from both public and total support if they meet certain criteria.[5]

(i) *Are attracted by reason of the publicly supported nature of the organization;*

(ii)*Are unusual or unexpected with respect to the amount thereof; and*

(iii) *Would by the reason of their size, adversely affect the status of the organization as normally meeting the one-third support test for any of the applicable periods described in paragraph*

The calculation should be done using **cash accounting.** However, generally accepted accounting principles require the accrual method of accounting. Some adjusting may be necessary if the preparer of Form 990 is using audited financial statements as the source of financial information, as these statements use accrual accounting. The first adjustment for

[5] Reg. 1.509(a)-3(c)(3) – Check line 28 on Schedule A, Part IV

unusual grants would be to remove the entry "grant receivable" from revenue because it is recorded but not actually received. The second adjustment would be to add back to revenue the amount received during the year, but classified as "deferred revenue.

Some disqualified donors will try giving their gifts to another public charity to keep the charitable contribution deduction on their personal income tax return. They then have the funds earmarked for the public charity from which they have been disqualified. There is a regulation that prohibits this kind of transaction, but discovery by the IRS is almost impossible.

SUMMARY OF THE FOUR TESTS:

Test #1 509(a)(1) The organization is described in 170(b)(1)(A)

i	a church or association of churches
ii	an educational organization
iii	medical or hospital
iv	in support of a state college
v	a governmental unit
vi	33&1/3% public support
	or facts & circumstances test

Test #2 509(a)(2) Public Support Tests:

more than one-third test

Numerator = permitted sources
Denominator = total support that is not
                      disqualified
                      less than one-third test:
Net U.B.I. + Investment Income
Total support that is not disqualified

Test #3 509(a)(3) Public charity status because of relationship to another public charity such as a church, IRS Income Tax Regulation 1.6033-2(g)(1)(vii).

Test #4 509(a)(4) Testing for public safety

Chapter 8

ACCOUNTING FOR SOLID WASTE MANAGEMENT

WHAT IS THE ROLE OF THE CERTIFIED PUBLIC ACCOUNTANT IN THE ENVIRONMENTAL DEBATE?

By
Jack E Bower, CPA
Associate Professor of Accounting
Eastern University
&
Jonathan E. Bower
Waste Management Specialist
Pennsylvania Department of Environmental Protection[1]

[1] Jonathan E. Bower is a Waste Management Specialist in the Waste Management Program of the Pennsylvania Department of Environmental Protection (DEP). Opinions and interpretations expressed in this article regarding environmental laws do not necessarily represent DEP's position on the law or enforcement of the law and should not be taken as a substitute for directly contacting DEP with questions and concerns. The DEP Southeast Regional Office is located at Lee Park, 555 North Lane, Conshohocken, PA 19428. 1 Costanza, Robert, Ecological Economics: The Science and Management of Sustainability, Columbia U. Press, N.Y. 1991

I. BACKGROUND

A significant group of scholars have addressed the need for more National Income Accounting measures that will track the dangers of economic over expansion.[2] This chapter focuses on the role of the Certified Public Accountant as auditor and/or consultant in the environmental debate regarding solid waste management.

The environment is a capital asset and a factor of production to all industries. For certain industries there is an ascertainable environmental degradation as a consequence of their method of production. Most noticeable is the planet's limited capacity to absorb waste. Proper waste management is a recognized responsibility mandated by society and enforced the by Environmental Protection Agency (EPA) and state agencies such as the Department of Environmental Protection (DEP)[3]. When discovered, the failure of a company to properly manage waste or the release of contaminants can result in significant fines and penalties (enforcement actions) to both the company and the accountant for violations of state and federal regulations.[4]

The proper management of waste is highly regulated and is therefore a costly and increasingly

---

[2] In 1980 the Comprehensive Environmental Response, Compensation, and Liability Act (CERCLA) was passed by the U.S. Congress. The legislation authorized the federal government to hold polluters financially responsible for cleanup costs.

[3] Andrews, Andrea; Simonetti, Gilbert, *Litigation/Management Accounting: Tort Reform Revolution.* A.I.C.P.A., Journal of Accountancy, September 1996, 9-96 J.A. 53. Also see, *Accountants Liability,* Practicing Law Institute, 1:2 Services Commonly Performed by Accountants & Chapter 2, Standards of the Accounting Profession, Copyright 2001.

[4] Full Cost Accounting in Action: Case Studies of Six Solid Waste Management Agencies, EPA, Solid Waste and Emergency Response, December 1998.

more complex process[5]. The financial impact of a non-compliant waste activity can potentially be a material item for any company and, thus, a potential unrecorded liability. It is only a matter of time until more and more responsibility for reporting the environmental liabilities comes under the scope of an audit. Even now, the A.I.C.P.A. "General Procedures" checklist instructs auditors to "obtain an understanding of the effect of laws, regulations, and ordinances having a direct and material effect on the financial statements, and prepare a list of such laws and regulations and attach it to the audit program."[6] Audit programs such as *Practitioners Clearing House* instructs auditors to determine *"Has the entity violated environmental laws? Does the entity use or generate "regulated substances" in its business?"*[7]

Accountants are familiar with depreciation, amortization and depletion. The consumption of environmental assets is called "environmental deterioration" and "resource consumption." Larger companies might employ an environmental health and safety director, a biophysical analyst, who estimates the damage or deterioration. Smaller companies can hire one of the many environmental consultants knowledgeable in biophysical analysis. These individuals can assign a dollar value to resource consumption and can recommend proper disposal

[5] General Procedures, Program aam54020.pgm, Copyright 1996 A.I.C.P.A. Inc.

[6] General Procedures, Audit Objectives, Practitioners Clearing House, Fort Worth, TX, Feb. 2000.

[7] Sunoco, Inc., 2005 *Health and Environment & Safety Review and CERES Report.* For more information on CERES (Coalition for Environmentally Responsible Economics) go to http://www.ceres.org ISO 14000 Info Center: www.iso14000.com. Rezaee, Z. Help Keep the World Green, *Journal of Accountancy*, November 2000, #57.

methods. Some companies also establish an environmental policy. For example, Sunoco Inc. utilizes the CERES principles, which "establish an environmental ethic with criteria by which investors and others can assess the environmental performance of the company."[8] Proper management of waste is critical to reducing costs. It is always more cost effective in the long run to properly handle and lawfully dispose of waste then to pay the fines and undergo remediation penalties. If an audit forces the company to address environmental issues ahead of time the savings can be significant.

The International Organization for Standardization (ISO) encourages auditors to undergo ISO 14000 training and certification so they will be able to examine environmental management systems (EMS). ISO 14000 is a proactive approach to managing environmental problems and risks and also seeks to integrate EMS into a company's overall internal control structure. As consultants, auditors can play a critical role in voluntary compliance (compliance assistance) by assisting a company in obtaining ISO 14000 Environmental Standards Certification. The EMS audit tests "compliance with both internal and external laws, regulations and policies." The goal is to improve an organization's environmental performance by reducing resource consumption and pollution of all kinds and by protecting the environment.

[8] Cox, Robert M. Jr., *Tough Environmental Regulations Bring New Opportunities for CPA's*, Pennsylvania CPA Journal, Summer 2001. Willits, S. D., and Metil, M. G. "Eco-audits examine operations to find ways to avoid environmental problems and to conserve resources." In, "Roles for CPA's in Clients' Eco-Audits," *Pennsylvania CPA Journal*, December 1996.

II. AUDIT PROCEDURES:

The key issues for auditors are (1) recognition of the environmental risk factors and (2) determining compliance with the proper requirements.[9] Properly handling and recording an organization's waste streams is a preventive action, in contrast to the materially significant, unrecorded liabilities just waiting to explode into a major environmental incident.

For the accountant, the first step in planning is an increased awareness of the creation of waste products. The insightful accountant will see everything as a process. Every item that is manufactured, repaired and every service that interacts with the physical world is a process that creates some type of waste. Even those industries in the business of knowledge management or knowledge creation produce a paper waste. Businesses that generate problematic types of waste can be small operations such as a veterinarian or an auto dealership. Both produce waste products that require special types of disposal.

The first audit procedure in finding an unrecorded waste liability is a review of the bills or "disposal receipts" and "waste manifests." The cost of proper waste disposal is usually expensive. Does the client show an expense for waste disposal other than the local trash company? Household waste called "Municipal Waste" and construction and demolition "C&D" waste require less tracking. Other types of waste, such as industry waste, processing waste and hazardous waste

[9] Klavens, Jonathan S. Esq., Chair; Clack, Holly A. CPA; Koch, Gayle CPA; McCaffery Maura; Newell, John O. Esq., Environmental Disclosure, When and How to Disclose Environmental Matters Under SEC and Accounting Requirements, Massachusetts Continuing Legal Education, Inc. 2000.

require a paper trail to ensure the removal of liability as a result of proper disposal. The liability is removed when the company can document proper disposal. The paper trail can consist of disposal receipts, biennial reports, waste determinations, land disposal restriction forms and return manifests signed by a disposal facility.

A paid invoice for waste disposal, however, is not always sufficient evidence to avoid liability. A returned receipt (signed manifest) from a proper disposal site is required to insure lawful disposal for certain types of waste. This is because the original generator of the waste (generating facility) is still responsible for disposal after the waste removal or shipping company has been paid. If the waste-removal or shipping company improperly disposed of the waste, the EPA can name the generating facility as a "Partially Responsible Party" or (PRP). This is the term used by the EPA when assigning a liability for remedial action. Companies have been successfully fined years after they paid for proper disposal because they thought they sent their waste to a properly "permitted" disposal site. The shipping company as low bidder may have generated extra revenue for itself by using an improper disposal site. The key audit issue is the existence of this signed and dated "Generator Return Copy" from the original shipping manifest, which confirms proper disposal. Pennsylvania uses a hazardous waste six part form called the "Transfer Storage Disposal Manifest." The six copies are routed as follows:

1. A copy is sent to the D.E.P.
2. A copy is sent to the state government of the generating facility such as New Jersey or Delaware if the disposal site is in PA.

3. A copy is signed by storage/disposal site and returned to the generating facility.
4. A copy is retained by the storage/disposal site.
5. A copy is retained by the transporter.
6. The original copy is retained by generator of the waste

In the event of contamination, the administrative authority such as the DEP will attempt to identify all those within the appropriate region who generate the substance or chemical agent causing the contamination. These generators might be required to submit copies of returned manifests along with additional information showing the amount of waste generated by each production process. Without the return copy, the company can be held as a PRP. The cost to the responsible parties or PRPs can be enormous. If ground water is contaminated, for example, the costs might include a new public water system for the affected area. Most matters are litigated, so resolution of the extent of the fines and remediation usually depend on a court order.

Waste disposal can also be a management letter item. Ideally, ways and means to reduce or eliminate waste should be sought for every waste-producing process. For example, substituting a less volatile chemical may increase chemical purchase costs but lower environmental risk and disposal costs. Such substitution is what the state of Pennsylvania calls a "source reduction strategy" or what accountants call an eco-audit. As another example, trucks now cleaned with a solvent-based cleaner can be cleaned with a citric-based cleaner that requires fewer disposal costs and less record keeping. A source reduction strategy might provide incentive for a company to hire a health and safety officer or an environmental hygienist to begin the process. In the long run, the cost savings could be significant

III. GUIDANCE FROM THE FASB, SFAS 5 AND STATEMENT OF POSITION 96-1.[10]

In accounting for remediation, uncertainty reigns supreme! All of the parties associated with an environmental problem could potentially be liable for the cost of the cleanup-even if their contribution to the problem was very small. Before accepting significant financial responsibility, a company will negotiate, and—depending on the amount—pursue a legal defense over the allocation of the cost between the involved parties. This is the first major uncertainty. The second major uncertainty is the actual cost of the cleanup. Preliminary remediation studies can yield vastly different results. The cost of the clean up will not be known with any degree of certainty until a detailed site remediation plan can actually assess the extent of the damage.

As a result of the financial uncertainty and prolonged negotiations, most companies will resist recording a financial liability even when named as a responsible party for fear that it will show an acknowledgement of guilt. Accounting rules support this position as long as particular uncertainties exist. Statement of Position 96-1[11] and SFAS 5 require that

[10] Trott, Edward., Chair of the Environmental Accounting Task Force said the SOP has omitted a discussion of the measurement of the legal cost of the remediation liability, "from the comment letters this was the most contentious issue." Journal of Accounting, October 1996, page 17.

[11] Mary E. Barth, Maureen F. McNichols, and G. Peter Wilson, 1997, "Factors Influencing Firms' Disclosure about Environmental Liabilities," Review of Accounting Studies 2, (1):35-64.

an obligation be reported when the following conditions are met:
1. A company has been identified as a potentially responsible party.
2. The company is participating in a remedial feasibility study.
3. A remedial feasibility study has been completed.
4. The cleanup method has been decided and cleanup costs have been estimated.
5. The firm has been ordered to clean up a site.

The auditor is faced with a conflict between full disclosure, FASB guidance and the goals of management. Certainly the allocation of cost uncertainty, litigation and negotiation concerns will dominate the disclosure conversation between management and the auditor.[12] This is another area that requires risk management by the auditor.

IV. JOURNAL ENTRIES AND ABC.

In most situations, there are four levels of environmental costs that are important from an accounting perspective:[13]
1. Usual Costs of Operation such as disposal costs, which perhaps are not recognized but should be recognized.
2. Hidden Regulatory Costs inclusive of reporting, permitting, monitoring, testing,

---

[12] Bailey, Paul. *Full Cost Accounting for Life-Cycle Costs – A Guide for Engineers and Financial Analysts,* Environmental Finance, spring 1991.

[13] Kreuze, Jerry G. CPA and Newell, Gale, CMA, *ABC and Life-Cycle Costing for Environmental Expenditures,* Management Accounting, February 1994, 38 to 42.

training and inspection.[14]

3. Contingent Liability Costs inclusive of penalties and fines for noncompliance, legal fees and settlement amounts for remedial actions, personal injuries and property damage.

4. A cost savings also might be realized from lower marketing costs as a result of increased consumer demand for environmentally friendly products, improved consumer satisfaction, improved employee relations and improved corporate image.

The major issue from a cost-control perspective is the proper allocation of costs to activities and then to products. Operations, which produce products and use Activity - Based Costing (ABC), will be more likely to attempt to properly allocate environmental costs to the products that cause environmental problems.

From an audit perspective, it is the lack of awareness and/or estimation of costs that generates audit risk. Most states keep extensive records of historical violations per generator. Auditors would be well advised to check state records when auditing a client with known violations or discharge areas on the site. In Pennsylvania the auditor should check: www.dep.state.pa.us, Subjects, eFacts, and then perform a search under the eFacts database.

V. A CHRISTIAN PERSPECTIVE

Where should Christians stand on environmental issues? Certainly the Scriptures are clear that the

[14] Trott, Edward., Chair of the Environmental Accounting Task Force said the SOP has omitted a discussion of the measurement of the legal cost of the remediation liability, "from the comment letters this was the most contentious issue." Journal of Accounting, October 1996, page 17.

universe and everything in it belongs to God. The Scriptures also teach that we are accountable to God for being stewards of His creation (Genesis 1:27-28). And God promises, "I will send you rain in its season, and the ground will yield its crops and the trees of the field their fruit..." (Leviticus 26:4-5, New International Version). What has emerged in the environmental debate is the age-old problem of confusing the order of creation with God Himself. From the beginning of time, mankind has falsely assigned god-like qualities to nonspiritual objects and then worshiped them as gods. The term "mother nature" refers to the complex ecosystems created by God to maintain order and balance on the earth. This is similar to the concept of giving "good luck" the credit for blessings instead of recognizing God's providence at work in our lives. Unfortunately, for many individuals "mother nature" has become the same as God and has become the source of all values. To these individuals, man is the intruder. Environmental decisions are made only in terms of what is best for nature.

Some members of the religious community have responded to the idolatry of making "mother nature" a god and other misperceptions with a doctrinal statement called the "Cornwall Declaration on Environmental Stewardship." The statement received its name from West Cornwall, Connecticut, where leading scholars from the Jewish, Catholic and Protestant community came together in October 1999 to craft an interfaith statement of common concerns and beliefs regarding environmental stewardship. Their statement can be found at .

Not far from West Cornwall, Connecticut, is the coastal town of Mystic, Connecticut, which illustrates the environmental debate. The town is a working model of a recreated 17th-century whaling community. The curators of Mystic describe in detail the risks and rewards of hunting and killing whales for their blubber, which was turned into oil for lamps. In hunting whales, harpoons were attached with rope to a small boat. When the hunters harpooned a whale, the whale towed the boat until the whale was exhausted. At the end of ride, the whale was butchered for its fat. Many sailors and many whales lost their lives on the "Nantucket slay ride." Why? Because from whales, humans wanted a product that advanced the human condition and economic progress.

Here is the dilemma. In the name of economic progress and an increased standard of living, the environment is destroyed. But the advancements from economic progress often can solve environmental problems just as the light bulb and electric power ended the slaughter of whales for their fat. Man is a consumer of the environment, but is simultaneously a creator who adds to the earth's abundance. What gift of new technology will God give to us to solve our fossil fuel shortage? Will God send oblivion to the human race by ultraviolet radiation penetrating through a hole in the ozone layer, or will He send deliverance in the form of a new technology? Not very many years ago, scientists predicted that everyone in northern climates would freeze to death for the lack of coal or firewood. Since the fall of Adam and Eve, humankind—whether individuals acknowledge it or not—has always been dependent upon God for deliverance from ourselves.

Is the environmental crisis real? Yes, it is real! The largest life forms on planet earth live in the rainforests of the Hoh River Valley in Washington's Olympic National Park. It takes five people touching hands to circle the base of one tree. Standing three hundred feet tall, these trees began life at about the time Jesus was born. Virgin forests were common in the United States and around the world about 1000 years ago. Not today. The virgin forests from Maine to North Carolina and west to the Mississippi have been reduced by 98%. The destruction of virgin forests worldwide constitutes a major environmental disaster in terms of clean water; clear air; flood control; and healthy, diverse ecosystems. In Haiti, for example, most of the forests have been consumed. Now each rainy season, more and more tillable soil washes off the rocks and out into the ocean. For the poor, there is no wood for fuel to cook food and no clean, uncontaminated water. The situation is grim and getting worse. Replacement forests, if we had room for them, would for many years lack the ability to retain soil, produce oxygen and function as watersheds. New York City, for example, depends on the watershed of the Catskill Mountains for clean water. Destroy the forests of the Catskills, and spend billions of dollars to provide NYC with clean water. Lost forests are only one example of the environmental crisis.

What are the solutions? Some believe it is the United Nations' responsibility to form a sort of international environmental protection agency. Most noteworthy was the United Nations Convention on Climate Change and the Kyoto Protocol Treaty, which is facing consideration by 150 industrial nations. The treaty would regulate the reduction of "man-made greenhouse gases in the atmosphere, such as carbon dioxide, by a total of about 5% overall—based on 1990 levels—between 2008 and 2012." In the U.S., for example, the Kyoto Protocol Treaty calls for a reduction of 7%, and critics estimate the cost to the

U.S. at $300 billion per year. The treaty would impact every industry that burns fuels. Of course, this depends on ratification and funding by Congress, and the treaty certainly has many opponents. Copies of the treaty, including background information, are available at . The official United Nations' site is . At the time this chapter was being written (Spring 2006), the position of the Bush Administration was to reject the Kyoto Protocol Treaty. The nation leading the lobbying effort for ratification is the U.K. This means the British leader Tony Blair has been in the U.S. trying to convince energy companies that there is profit in compliance with the provisions of the Kyoto Treaty. The Bush Administration is already spending "tens of millions of dollars each year developing the technology" to reduce and store carbon dioxide.[15] This technology would then be available for sale to developing countries. The position of the Bush Administration on Global-warming is the traditional Republican Party plank, individual company responsibility.

Other preservationists believe ecotourism is part of the answer. Charging tourists to visit and play in the natural ecosystems is saving some natural areas. It has worked well for Costa Rica and Puerto Rico. Some nations use the resulting funds to retire the national debt at reduced rates in return for preserving natural areas.

Dozens of other ideas exist. The solutions are a matter of perspective. All of us who live, eat and breathe on this planet need to respect it. We need to see it as a part of our future. We need to see the interdependence of the biosphere. We need to recognize

[15] Mary E. Barth, Maureen F. McNichols, and G. Peter Wilson, 1997, "Factors Influencing Firms' Disclosure about Environmental Liabilities," Review of Accounting Studies 2, (1):35-64.

our responsibility for the stewardship of God's creation. In all of these perspectives, Christians should take the lead, working as if it depends on our actions and praying as if it depends on God's grace for new technologies.

TABLE I.
TYPES OF DISPOSABLE WASTE

Residual waste: non hazardous waste created by a process

Municipal waste: household waste, C & D waste and infectious waste

Hazardous waste: Listed in Title 40 – Protection of the Environment, (C.F.R.), EPA, Chapter 1, section 261.31 & 32 (PA, for example, has adopted the federal regulation for the definition of hazardous waste. Some states have taken a more stringent approach.) There are basically four characteristics of substances that qualify them as hazardous waste:

1. Ignitability: Wastes that can readily catch fire and sustain combustion such as paints and cleaners.
2. Corrosivity: Wastes that are acidic or alkaline such as sulfuric acid from automotive batteries.
3. Reactivity: Wastes that readily explode or undergo violent reactions such as discarded munitions or explosives.
4. Toxicity: Wastes that leach dangerous concentrations of toxic chemicals into the ground water.

TABLE II.
REFERENCE MATERIALS

Measuring Corporate Environmental Performance: Best Practices for Costing and Measuring an Effective Environmental Strategy. By Marc J. Epstein, Ph.D. Co-published by Irwin and the Institute of Management Accountants Foundation for Applied Research, 1997.

Advances in Environmental Accounting & Management. Edited by Martin Freedman and Bikki Jaggi. Published by an imprint of Elsevier Science, 2000.

Environmental Disclosure: When and How to Disclose Environmental Matters Under SEC and Accounting Requirements. Published by Massachusetts Continuing Legal Education, 2000.

Contemporary Environmental Accounting Issues, Concepts and Practice. By Stefan Schaltegger and Roger Burritt. Published by Greenleaf Publishing, 2000. (This is a 462-page environmental accounting textbook.)

Title 40 – Protection of the Environment, Chapter 1. Known as "40 CFR." This Federal Law title details all the federal laws related to environmental protection. The major parts dealing with hazardous waste management and the functioning of the agency are parts

260 to 299. Like the Internal Revenue Code, this is a massive amount of material to read. Parts 260 to 265 are more than 500 pages long.

RCRA Orientation Manual. Published by the EPA. The EPA says the manual "has proven to be a popular and valuable resource for anyone working with the EPA's solid and hazardous waste." Available from the U.S. Environmental Protection Agency, Office of Solid Waste/Communications, Information, and Resources Management Division, 401 M Street, SW, Washington, D.C. 20460.

Pennsylvania Code, Title 25. Environmental Protection, Department of Environmental Protection. This is *the* major source of environmental law in Pennsylvania. Residual Waste Management is covered in one book from chapters 287 through 299. Municipal Waste Management is dealt with in chapters 271 through 285 and is covered in another book. Each chapter is about 100 pages long and is significantly more readable than federal code sections. Available from the Department of Environmental Protection, Bureau of Land Recycling and Waste Management, Division of Municipal and Residual Waste, Rachel Carson State Office Building, 14th floor, 400 Market Street, Harrisburg, PA 17105-8472. Phone: (717) 787-7381. Each of the code books will list a date for which it is current through a certain Pennsylvania Bulletin (Pa. B.). Similar to federal publications such as *The Cumulative Bulletin* of the federal government, readers must consult the Pa. B. for the current law. The Pa. B. is available from Fry Communications Inc., 800 W. Church Rd., Mechanicsburg, PA 17055-3198. For example, Pa. B. Vol. 29, Number 18, provides an update on the Environmental Quality Board's hazardous waste regulation. Most regulations are also available from the DEP web site. Under subjects, go to "land recycling" and then "EFACTS."

Hazardous Waste Management. By Michael D. LaGrega, Phillip Buckingham & Jeffrey C. Evans. Published by McGraw Hill Inc., 1994. In more than 1000 pages, the authors examine current management practices, treatment and disposal methods, as well as site remediation. The book is highly recommended as the leader in the field.

Dappern, A., and Johnson, R. 2000, Dec. Taking a stand. *Hemispheres*: 107.

Sauer, L. J. 1998. *The Once and Future Forest*. Washington, D.C.: Island Press.

The United Nations has a problem getting consensus on environmental issues. For example, the "Report by the Expert Working Group Meeting on Improving Governments' Role in the Promotion of Environmental Managerial Accounting" reports, "There is no consensus on the scope, content, or procedures of Environmental Managerial Accounting" (Division for Sustainable Development, 2000).

Fialka, J. J. 2000, Nov. 27. "Climate talks are suspended amid deadlock." Wall Street Journal: A3.

The Global Climate Coalition (an industry PAC) offers a critical view of the Kyoto Protocol Treaty. For articles explaining opposition to the treaty, see the *Chemical Week* Web site or *The American City Business Journals Inc.*

The Kyoto Protocol Treaty is available to the public by contacting the National Council for Science and the Environment, 1725 K Street, NW, Suite 212, Washington, D.C. 20006. Phone number: (202) 530-5810.

Chapter 9

THE MARRIAGE OF LOVE AND GREED

AN ANGLO-SAXON ROMANCE

By
Dr. Jack E. Bower, CPA
Associate Professor of Accounting
Eastern University

The title question begs a discussion of many topics. To narrow the field, a few definitions and historical background information are in order. This is not a chapter on political theory, which addresses the relationship of the state to the individual, the role of the church or political authority. It is not a discussion of the separation of church and state. It is an attempt to explain why two value systems, one based on self-interest (capitalism) and the other (Christianity) based on an interest in others (love), exist so excellently together from a historical perspective. It is perfectly clear from the history of nations that neither capitalism nor democracy needs each other to exist.

But, add Christianity to the mix and they tend to flourish, why? The simple explanation has always been that Christianity creates the perfect moral climate for both capitalism and democracy. While I acknowledge that this is true for democracy, there is a fundamental disconnect between Christianity based on a principle of love for others and capitalism based on the principle of self-interest. I believe, however that these two opposing systems, Christianity and capitalism, share a common set of ideological principles, the principles of liberty.[1] I will begin with a brief historical critique of capitalism followed by a brief analysis of democracy. The last part of the chapter will address the shared principles of liberty.

Our definition of Anglo-Saxon capitalism is traditional.[2] It is not my goal to redefine capitalism, defend it or criticize it. The traditional definition of capitalism is that individuals should be free to work on their own behalf, towards self-interest, for their own happiness. This means a freedom to trade with others who have the same willingness to trade, what I commonly call free markets. The economic roots of capitalism are ancient. The Bible, from Genesis to Revelation tells us about a significant number of economic exchanges that follow the principles of capitalism. A good example would be the purchase of Sarah's burial cave by Abraham in Genesis 23 or the perhaps the offer to the Shechemites to acquire

[1] The idea for this chapter came from a Bible class taught by Mark Pagenkopf at the King of Prussia church of Christ, KOP, PA.

[2] Germany's Social Democrats and the French refer to the current form of capitalism practiced in the U.S. and Britain as Anglo-Saxon Capitalism, Financial Times, Wednesday June 15, 2005, page 1, comments made by John Snow, U.S. Treasury Secretary, *"Treasury secretary decries anti-capitalist rhetoric."*

holdings in Genesis 34. Jesus used the example of trading (buying low and selling high) in Luke 19 and makes reference to profit in verse 15. Traders and profit are also mentioned in Revelation 18:16. Capitalism generally requires the right to act as legal persons and is based on the ownership of private property.

Critical analysis of capitalism became a significant issue about the 13th century as capitalism started to become a powerful economic force (more traders and less farmers). Was it a sinful activity to profit at the expense of others? Thomas Aquinas (1225 to 1275) was the first of this era to address the rise of capitalism. Some scholars refer to him as the first economist. He addressed the major issue of buying low and selling high, was it a sin? His answer was no, as long as profit was limited to a "just" profit.[3] There is considerable evidence to suggest that Thomas Aquinas used creation and the dual nature of God to create the modern double entry accounting system in use today as the means of calculating profit.

The next major church critic was Martin Luther, who lived from 1483 to 1546. At least one scholar *"has demonstrated conclusively, Luther was seriously searching for a new economic ethic. He undermined the Catholic system of almsgiving and beggary. He struggled unsuccessfully for effective ways to oppose an emerging capitalism"*[i] Martin Luther is not known for his economic theories but he was worried about the greed generated by a capitalist economy. What he advocated was the U.S. Republican Party's primary platform plank, individual responsibility. Tony Campolo, Professor emeritus at Eastern University

[3] Chafuen, Alejandro, Faith and Liberty, Economic Thought of the Late Scholastics, Lexington Books, N.Y.2003, page 116.

says the story of the "Good Samaritan" in Luke 10:29ff is a story of the good Republican, individual responsibility for the welfare of others. Being himself a Democrat, Professor Campolo says the Democrats would have built a tollbooth on the road from Jerusalem to Jericho, installed lighting, hired police, and the mugging would never have happened in the first place. Luther *"envisioned the Christians as offering love and enacting justice for the neighbor by means of honest work, in the duties of one's calling."*[4]

Clearly the most recognized critic of capitalism was Karl Marx who lived from 1818 to 1883. He believed that the owners of capital would profit at the expense of the workers and definitely would exploit them if allowed to do so. The legendary literary work of Marx is called *The Communist Manifesto*, first published in 1848. The co-author was Friedrich Engels. It is one of the most historically influential political documents in human history. He argues that the very structure of capitalism will lead to exploitation even in a democracy. (Perhaps he was familiar with the economic exploitation of Jacob by Laban in Genesis 29, but not how God turned it into profit.) Some Christians find support for Marxism in Acts 2:44 *"and all who shared the faith owned everything in common."*

Marx failed to anticipate two things. First, the capital deepening that was made possible by ever evolving technology. Capital deepening increased the productivity of workers and made it possible for wages to increase even as output increased. Expanding capital did not experience diminishing returns and owners did not have to "steal" wages from workers in order to maintain profits. What Marx also failed to see

[4] Rieth, Ricardo Willy, Luther on Greed, Lutheran Quarterly, Vol. XV, 2001

was the evolution of a third class of persons, what I call "management." They are not workers and not owners of the corporation for which they work, but act for the mutual benefit of both. The leading writer detailing the formation of this new class is Alfred Chandler in his book The Visible Hand: The Managerial Revolution in American Business, (a Pulitzer Prize winning book). He called the development of this new management class "a managerial revolution." The turning point according to Chandler was 1850, which began "managerial capitalism."

Ironic as it may seem, for the U.S., what Karl Marx advocated has actually happened. Over time as involvement in the shares market has grown, the workers have become the actual owners. Ordinary citizens through their defined contribution plans (401(k) plans) and their defined benefit plans own the majority shares of large publicly traded corporations. In real financial terms, the workers are increasingly the owners!

What has motivated the critics of capitalism is the very real potential for unbridled self-interest or what I commonly call greed. All of the critics and even the advocates of capitalism such as John Maynard Keynes (1883 to 1946), one of the most important economists of the century, believed and taught that greed was wrong, a vice. His famous work was *The General Theory of Employment, Interest and Money* written in 1936. Greed is never having enough, never enough money or land or power. For most of the history of capitalism, greed was a sin, a trap to be avoided. Perhaps Jesus said it best, *"Watch out! Be on your guard against all kinds of greed: for a man's life does not consist in the abundance of his possessions."* Luke 12:15. Then in 1987 came the movie "Wall Street" staring Michael Douglas as

Gordon Gecko who addressed the shareholders of the Teldar Paper Corporation. **Greed is Good**, said Mr. Gecko, and the phrase became the mantra of Wall Street. There are countless articles and even monthly columns about corporate shares that will make you rich, all under the title greed is good.

So what is democracy? Listening to the news, it is clearly many different things to many different people around the world. Most would agree that it means a complex set of individual freedoms and responsibilities, and of course the right to elect government representation. Some would argue that it means equality, suffrage, and freedom of speech. The U.S. Declaration of Independence, viewed by most persons as a document of democracy, claims the right to "life, liberty, and the pursuit of happiness." As mentioned in the opening paragraph, some scholars have properly argued that Christianity supports the social capital necessary for democracy and capitalism to exist so Ill together. Social capital is the moral consensus that generally underlies an enforceable system of laws regulating exchanges on a fair basis. It is this moral consensus (e.g., trust, honesty, hard work) that Weber recognized as the underpinnings of the rise of capitalism. This system of values lowers transaction costs and encourages specialization and productivity. It is the counter balance to greed. There is considerable truth to this argument. The most notable current scholar in this field of study is Robert H. Nelson with his book Economics as Religion. But, I believe that the support of social capital is not the complete story.

The U.S. is a complex example of economics as religion because it is a collection of many different states. Some of the original states (colonies) such as the Massachusetts Bay Colony based their democratic principles on Christian principles. Most of the other colonies Ire not based on Christianity as the dominant religion; hence the endless debate over the proper role of religion and government. It is note worthy to mention that the famous expression "separation of church and state" is not in the U.S. constitution. It is a judicial interpretation of the first amendment "Congress shall make no law respecting an establishment of religion" based upon a letter written by Thomas Jefferson. Unfortunately, most people think that the separation of church and state concept was a legislative act voted upon by people elected to represent the citizens of this nation. It is an example of the power of the judicial branch of government to shape and determine American culture. The same is true of the abortion issue. The U.S. form of democracy has three branches of government each with significant power to set standards of legal conduct and influence cultural norms.

The critical question is does democracy require Christianity? Does Capitalism require democracy? The answer is clearly no to both questions, they do not need each other to exist or co-exist. Capitalist systems have functioned well in Hong Kong, Singapore or Chile where the government is not elected. In the same way, democracy is not based on religion. The Ancient Greeks proved that a long time ago. Even the American concepts of a democratic republic are based on concepts of liberty that predated Christianity. But the question remains, why does capitalism and Christianity co-exist so well together when one is based on self interest and the other based on an interest in others; dipolar points of view?

I believe a significant part of the answer is the principles of liberty.[5] It is the common element that weaves the two together and allows for their excellent co-existence. Christianity supports liberty. Liberty supports democracy. Democracy supports Capitalism. Consider seven principles of Liberty that support democracy:

Liberty requires a sacrifice – even unto death in military service.

Liberty requires a commitment to something bigger than yourself, citizenship has responsibilities.

Liberty requires that a choice be made. "Give me *Liberty* or give me death, Patrick Henry, March 23, 1775.

The pursuit of liberty transforms life from one of contentment or self-indulgence to one of purpose. For example, the attack on our country on September 11 galvanized us as a nation to a common purpose.

Freedom is never free; it takes hard work and a constant vigilance to defend our liberty.

Freedom is always under attach by those who have a vested interest in bondage.

Under true liberty, all men are created equal.

How does Christianity also teach and support the same principles of liberty?

Christianity requires sacrifice – even unto death. "*I have been crucified with Christ and I no longer live, but Christ lives in me.*" Galatians 2:20 "*Who ever finds his life will lose it, and whoever loses his life for my sake*

---

[5] There are many lists of the principles of liberty. For example, some scholars believe that all liberty is of Divine Origin. Gowdy, David J., Institute for American Liberty. Reference is made to the scripture on the Liberty Bell, Leviticus 25:10 to prove this point.

will find it." Matthew 10:39

Christianity requires a commitment to something bigger than yourself. *"The life I live in the body, I live by faith in the Son of God, who loved me a gave himself for me."* Galatians 2:20. Faith in Jesus Christ requires total surrender and total commitment to the rule of Christ in our hearts. *"in view of God's mercy, to offer your bodies as living sacrifices, holy and pleasing to God."* Romans 12:1

Following God requires that a choice be made. *"choose for yourselves this day who you will serve."* Joshua 24:15. *"If anyone would come after me, he must deny himself and take up his cross and follow me."* Mark 8:34

The pursuit of being Christ like transforms life from one of contentment or self-indulgence to one of purpose. *"Do not conform any longer to the pattern of this world, but be transformed by the renewing of your minds."* Romans 12:1&2

Freedom is never free. *"I have fought the good fight, I have finished the race, I have kept the faith."* II Timothy 4:6

Freedom in Christ is always under attach by those who have a vested interest in bondage. *"Consider him who endured such opposition from sinful men, so that you will not grow weary and lose heart."* Hebrews 12:3

7. In Christ Jesus *"there is neither Jew nor Greek, slave nor free, male nor female,*

for you are all one in Christ Jesus." Galatians 3:28

Why do capitalism and Christianity co-exist so comfortable? They are both based on similar principles of liberty. Citizens who embrace the principles of Christianity are quick to embrace the principles of liberty. The founding of many of the U.S. colonies are good examples. They wanted religious freedom. But does the reverse hold true? Does the spread of liberty advance the spread of Christianity? Will the spread of liberty in the Middle East under the George W. Bush administration advance the Christian faith? Unlike the religion of Islam, Christianity rejects theocracy. Will the principles of liberty introduced to the Iraqi people over time draw a significant number of them to a faith in Jesus Christ? It would be great to do historical case studies on liberty and the spread of Christianity. The problem is the number of external factors. For example, the fastest growing religion in Kazakhstan is Christianity. Is this a result of their new liberty or just the filling of a spiritual void? What about the extensive growth of Christianity is in the Southern Hemisphere in recent years. A host of projections claim that in twenty years two thirds of all Christians will live in Africa, Latin America or Asia.[6] It seems that Christianity is returning to its geographic roots. It is difficult to correlate liberty and Christianity to prove if the liberty begets Christianity. What I do know is that the reverse is true. Christians, if given the opportunity, will choose liberty and in turn, this why capitalism based on greed, also supported by liberty, works Ill in a Christian context. The principles of liberty are the glue that holds it all together.

[6] Jenkins, Philip, *The Next Christendom: The Coming of Global Christianity,* Penn State U. Press. or Carpenter, Joel, *The Changing face of Christianity,* Calvin College.

Bibliography

Chafuen, Alejandro A., Faith and Liberty, The economic Thought of the Late Scholastics, Lexington Books, N.Y. 2003.

Chandler, Alfred. The Visible Hand: A Managerial Revolution. Belknap Press of Harvard U.

Daly, Herman and Cobb, John Jr., *For The Common Good*, Beacon Press, Boston, 1994.

Pemberton, Prentiss and Finn, Daniel Rush, Towards A Christian Economic Ethic, Winston Press, Minnesota, 1985.

Rieth, Ricardo Willy, Luther on Greed, Lutheran Quarterly, Vol.XV, 2001

Sider, Ronald, Just Generosity, Baker Books, MI, 1999.

Nelson, Robert, Economics as Religion, from Samuelson to Chicago and Beyond, The Pennsylvania State University Press, PA, 2001

Cobb, John Jr., Sustaining the Common Good, Pilgrim Press, Ohio, 1994.

American Rhetoric: Movie speech, Wall Street, 1987. Gordon Gekko's address to the shareholders of Teldar Paper.

Keynes, John Maynard, *The General Theory of Employment, Interest and Money* (1936).

PART IV

~ Accounting and Moral Philosophy

Chapter 10

THE MANNA PRINCIPLE:

TRUST THE PROVIDER
NOT THE PROVISION

By Daniel Fletcher[i]
Pulpit Minister, church of Christ
King of Prussia, PA

Please Read: Exodus 16:1-32, Luke 4:1-3, John 6:25-51 and 1 Timothy 6:17-19

INTRODUCTION:

Finances are fickle. The imagery of Proverbs 23:5 is worth noting: *"Cast but a glance at riches, and they are gone, for they will surely sprout wings and fly off to the sky like an eagle"* (NIV). Wealth cannot be trusted as a

[i] Daniel Fletcher is ABD for his PhD at Westminster Theological Seminary in Glenside, PA. He holds a B.A., M.A., and M.Div. from Lipscomb University in Nashville, TN.

source of security. That is a tough sell in today's consumer-oriented culture. Do we have much of a choice? After all, it seems as though money makes the world go around. For the most part, we do not live in a world where life's basic necessities are gathered naturally from the environment by individuals. We are not hunters and gatherers. These necessities are mass produced. So let's be honest, financial provision is essential for attaining these necessities. We need money for our day-to-day survival in a market-driven economy. God provides us with the skills necessary to earn material wealth so that we may contribute to society in a holy and responsible way. Therefore, material wealth (in moderation) is a basic need in today's world, and as such, comes from the hand of God. Although it is a basic need it is not the most essential need. After all, the Bible teaches us that wealth is not designed to last forever but rather to waste away.

The fact that God designs material wealth to rot away highlights the "manna principle." I use the term "manna" in a broad sense to include any **physical provision** of God; however, in keeping with a theme of finances, manna will be discussed in a financial context. So, the "manna principle" deals primarily, but not exclusively, with material wealth. *The manna principle deals with the attempt to hoard what is designed to rot away.* Note that there are two intertwined ideas here: 1) our ability to hoard, and 2) that which we hoard is designed to rot away. Jesus states it aptly,

> *"Do not store up for yourselves treasures on earth, **where moth and rust destroy,** and where thieves break in and steal. But store up for yourselves treasures in heaven, **where moth**

and rust do not destroy, *and where thieves do not break in and steal."* (Matt. 6:19-20)

Jesus' point is that material wealth is temporary. So then, the choice set before us, as God's people, is whether we will trust him as our Provider or the wealth he provides. *Will we trust the Provider or the provision?*

ANCIENT ISRAEL AND MANNA:

God provides for his people. Not only is he their creator but he is also their sustainer. God desires to provide for his people as a father provides for his children. God's point of view seems simple enough: he wants his people to trust him alone for their sustenance. Trusting God was one of the main lessons to be learned by the people of Israel as they wandered for forty years in the desert wilderness. Just as God brought them out of Egyptian bondage with a mighty hand, he desired to continue his care for them. The wilderness wandering was a forty year period of testing and discipline for the Israelites to see whether or not they would follow God's commands and if they would learn to trust in him alone as their provider (Deut. 8:2-5). It was the time of adolescence in Israel's history.[ii]

Exodus 16 records how God fed his people in the wilderness. Just as he satisfied their thirst (Exod. 15:23; 17:1-7) he also satisfied their hunger by miraculously providing manna and quail. *Manna*, a strange, heavenly bread, was said to be white like coriander seed and tasted like wafers made with honey

[ii] Peter Craigie, *The Book of Deuteronomy,* The New International Commentary on the Old Testament, (Grand Rapids: Eerdmans, 1976), 186.

(Exod. 16:31).[iii] The provision of manna was not a once-in-a-while occurrence meant to pacify the often grumbling Israelites, rather, it was a **daily** provision meant to instill trust in God, the creator and sustainer of his people (Exod. 16:4).[iv] The main purpose of sending manna was not simply to fill their stomachs nor was it expressly for the purpose of testing them. It was meant to teach them something about God.[v] With this miracle they would know that their God who brought them out of Egypt would continue his care for them (Exod. 16:6). The manna from heaven was the first great display of God's provision of food for his people in the wilderness. Israel would know that God is the great Provider.

The "manna principle" highlights an interesting characteristic of manna - it was **designed** to rot away at the end of the day. Manna was temporal in nature. God rained down a fresh supply of manna each day.[vi]

[iii] The word *manna* is derived from a Hebrew phrase which is translated, "What is it?" Though some scholars argue for the natural occurrence of manna, this questioning term highlights the miraculous nature of this bread from heaven. For more on this, see Peter Enns, *Exodus*, The NIV Application Commentary, (Grand Rapids: Zondervan, 2000), 326.

[iv] Incidentally, this daily occurrence may be a foundational influence on Jesus' words recorded in the Lord's Prayer, "Give us today our daily bread" (Matt. 6:11; Luke 11:3). For more on this idea, see Craig Keener, *A Commentary on the Gospel of Matthew*, (Grand Rapids: Eerdmans, 1999), 221-222.

[v] Enns, 325.

[vi] Moses commanded the Israelites to gather twice the usual amount of manna in preparation for the Sabbath day of rest. This lesson in dependence was for Israel to trust that God provided enough manna on the sixth day (Friday) to get them through each Sabbath. Since the Israelites were forbidden to work (i.e., gather manna) on the Sabbath, it was a day of *complete* dependence on God.

God instructed Moses to command the Israelites to gather only enough manna for each day, not keeping it until the morning (Exod. 16:19-24). In this, God tested the Israelites to see if they would trust him to provide for them each day or if they would rely on themselves for their daily sustenance. The simple fact that manna was designed to rot away was a test of Israel's faith.[vii] That is, *the test set before them was whether they would place their trust in their own ability to hoard manna, or whether they would place their trust in God to provide it afresh daily.* Knowing them to be a grumbling and insecure people (Exod. 15:24; 16:3), God sought to make them aware of their absolute reliance upon his gracious beneficence.[viii] He designed manna so that it would rot away eliminating Israel's temptation to hoard it. Israel had to trust God for their daily provision of manna.[ix]

Sadly, the Israelites failed repeatedly in the wilderness. They grumbled against Moses (Exod. 15:24; 16:3), they tried to hoard manna for themselves (Exod. 16:20), they tried to gather manna on the Sabbath (Exod. 27), they put God to the test (Exod. 17:3), and they made and worshiped an idol in the form of a golden calf (Exod. 32). The Israelites repeatedly sought autonomy from God, their Creator and Sustainer. They repeatedly failed to trust their Provider. Specifically, in their attempts to hoard manna overnight, as well as gather it on the Sabbath, the Israelites trusted themselves to provide, not the Provider. Similarly, they came to trust <u>what</u> was

[vii] Nahum Sarna, *Exodus,* The Jewish Publication Society Torah Commentary, (Philadelphia: The Jewish Publication Society, 1991), 89.
[viii] Ibid., 86.
[ix] Enns, 326.

provided rather than he who provided. In a very real sense, they came to believe that their ability to hoard manna was the source of their sustenance and survival in the wilderness. They failed the test by placing their trust in their own ability to hoard what was designed to rot away.

JESUS AND MANNA:

Jesus had his own experience with manna during his temptation in the wilderness. The Gospel of Luke records Jesus' wilderness experience in strikingly similar (and theologically significant) terms as Israel's (Luke 4:1-13). Not coincidentally, Jesus spent forty days in the wilderness, an obvious parallel to Israel's forty years. Israel was given the title "son" of God (Exod. 4:22; Hos. 11:1). The wilderness experience was a test to see if they would be an obedient son to their Father. But they failed miserably, succumbing to temptation after temptation. But in Luke, Jesus is presented as the true "Son" of God who lived out his life in obedience to the Father. Where Israel was a disobedient son, Jesus was obedient. Just as God led Israel through the wilderness where they failed, falling to every temptation, Jesus was also led by God (through the Holy Spirit) (Luke 4:1) into the wilderness, where he faced the same temptations but was successful.[x] Jesus is presented as the true Son of God, in whom the destiny of Israel was recapitulated and the divine purpose accomplished, in that he rendered to God the obedience and trust that Israel failed to give.[xi]

[x] Mark Black, *Luke,* The College Press NIV Commentary, (Joplin, Mo.: College Press Publishing Company, 1996), 98.
[xi] C. F. Evans, *Saint Luke,* The Trinity Press International New Testament Commentaries, (Philadelphia: Trinity Press International, 1990), 256.

After Jesus fasted for forty days, anticipating his hunger, the devil says to him, *"If you are the Son of God, tell this stone to become bread"* (Luke 4:3). The temptation here is not simply to miraculously provide food. There is nothing inherently sinful in this. After all, if this sort of miraculous act were sinful, Jesus would have sinned when he fed the five thousand in Luke 9:12-17. The primary temptation is to exploit his Sonship.[xii] The temptation is to use his divine empowerment to meet his own physical needs. It is the temptation to trust himself to provide rather than God. Thus, it is the same temptation faced by the Israelites in the wilderness when they tried to hoard manna. They sought to provide manna for themselves rather than trust that God would provide a fresh supply each day. In contrast, Jesus trusts the Father alone to provide for his needs.

Jesus' use of Scripture allows for a clear understanding of the nature of the temptation involved. He responds to this temptation by applying the manna narrative, as described in Deuteronomy 8:2-4, to his current situation. Quoting part of Deuteronomy 8:3, Jesus says, *"Man does not live on bread alone"* (Luke 4:3). Jesus' response is twofold. First, the principle behind this text, in both Deuteronomy and Luke, is **trust**. Jesus' response indicates that satisfying one's hunger by one's own initiative represents a distrust of God. *Jesus trusts God to provide more than in his own ability to provide for himself.* Jesus understands well that when facing a period of testing, our self-sufficiency is undermined, for our own ability to provide for our needs is removed and we learn that our existence, physical and spiritual, can only be grounded in God.[xiii] Jesus knows that God is the sustainer of his life, not himself. Second, Jesus' answer

---

[xii] John Nolland, *Luke 1-9:20,* Word Biblical Commentary, (Dallas: Word Books, 1989), 179.
[xiii] Craigie, 186.

highlights the role of hunger. Israel's hunger in the wilderness served a purpose, i.e., to help them understand that "one does not live by bread alone." Humans are not like mere animals, living only on the level of physical needs.[xiv] Rather, a personal and intimate knowledge of the living God brings true life. God caused the Israelites to hunger so they would come to understand that **he** was their sole source of life. *Manna does not satisfy, nor can it, for it is designed to rot away.* Israel failed to grasp this reality and tried to hoard manna, and in a sense, trusted in it to sustain them rather than God. So, another aspect of Jesus' temptation is to place his trust in that which perishes. *Jesus trusts the Provider not the provision.*

JESUS IS THE TRUE MANNA:

Jesus reinterprets the Old Testament manna story in John 6:25-51. At the expense of a detailed exposition of this passage,[xv] suffice it to say here that <u>Jesus</u> is the only provision from God that truly satisfies hunger and truly brings eternal life. He is the true manna that has been sent from heaven (John 6:32-33). The manna eaten by the Israelites in the wilderness was designed to rot away at the end of each day. It was designed to create a hunger that could only be satisfied by God. It was not true bread for it satisfied only temporarily.[xvi] But the bread that God provides today, through an intimate and enduring relationship with Jesus Christ,

[xiv] Leon Morris, *The Gospel According to St. Luke,* Tyndale New Testament Commentaries, (Grand Rapids: Eerdmans, 1979), 103.

[xv] For a detailed, yet practical discussion of this text in relation to its Old Testament counterpart, see Gary Burge, *John,* The NIV Application Commentary, (Grand Rapids: Zondervan, 2000), 197-216.

[xvi] Herman Ridderbos, *The Gospel of John,* (Grand Rapids: Eerdmans, 1997), 227.

satisfies **forever**. Jesus says concerning himself, the true manna, *"I am the bread of life. Whoever comes to me will never be hungry, and whoever believes in me will never be thirsty"* (John 6:35).

Jesus exhorts us to pursue the proper kind of bread in this life – that which does not spoil: *"Do not work for food that spoils, but for food that endures to eternal life, which the Son of Man will give you"* (John 6:27). The contrast that Jesus makes with material manna is obvious. Manna was designed to spoil at the end of the day which was meant to instill trust in God, the great Provider. Even today, our best efforts to provide material manna for ourselves fall miserably short of God's ideal. The material manna that we work for and strive to attain is designed by God to spoil. Not that we should cease to earn a material living in this market-driven economy (for that would be irresponsible), but we should keep a proper, holy perspective. Merely material notions of blessing are not worth pursuing.[xvii] Just like manna, the seductive appeal of material possessions evaporates.[xviii] Jesus wants us to realize that there is something far more enduring to work for – bread that does not spoil, that comes as a result of pursuing a trusting relationship with God. What we should "work for" is faith in Christ.[xix]

APPLICATION:

The apostle Paul applies the manna principle to the church in the context of stewardship. His words echo those of Jesus when he emphasizes the futility of trusting in material wealth:

[xvii] D. A. Carson, *The Gospel According to John,* The Pillar New Testament Commentary, (Grand Rapids: Eerdmans, 1991), 284.
[xviii] Burge, 210.
[xix] Carson, 285.

*"Command those who are rich in this present world not to be arrogant nor to put their hope in wealth, **which is so uncertain,** but to put their hope in God, who richly provides us with everything for our enjoyment. Command them to do good, to be rich in good deeds, and to be **generous and willing to share.** In this way they will lay up treasure for themselves as a firm foundation for the coming age, so that they may take hold of the life that is truly life."* (1 Tim. 6:17-19)

Here, Paul contrasts the certainty of God with the uncertainty of wealth. This is no abstract principle but rather one that should be applied in concrete situations. Material wealth is not only to be consumed but also distributed. Instead of simply hoarding wealth for our own needs we should also seek to use it to meet the needs of others. Paul's point is that just as God provides for our needs we should, in-turn, help provide for the needs of others. *We are to be distributors of God's gifts.* With God's gifts comes responsibility. God's material blessings are not ends in themselves but are to be used as instruments of creative expression that reflect the graciousness of God.[xx] Notice Paul's word play on "rich" throughout the passage – the *rich* are to be *rich* in generosity and good deeds.[xxi] To "do good" and to be "rich in good deeds" (1 Tim. 6:18) involves using wealth in a positive way to help others instead of letting it feed a life of personal luxury.[xxii]

[xx] Richard Cunningham, *Creative Stewardship,* (Nashville: Abingdon, 1979), 78.

[xxi] C. Michael Moss, *1, 2 Timothy & Titus,* The College Press NIV Commentary, (Joplin, MO.: College Press Publishing Company, 1994), 127.

[xxii] Thomas Lea and Hayne Griffin, Jr., *1, 2 Timothy & Titus,* The New American Commentary, Vol. 34, (Nashville: Broadman, 1992), 175.

Stewardship provides many opportunities for distributing material blessings. We can use these blessings for any purpose that cares for basic human needs or enriches and ennobles human life through the pursuit of godliness, the creation of beauty, or the struggle for human rights, justice, and dignity.[xxiii] To use wealth in these ways is to lay hold of "life that is truly life" (1 Tim. 6:19). Selfless and generous living, motivated by love, brings with it a future life in heaven.

CONCLUSION:

Our present experience in this world is not unlike Israel's or Jesus'. We live in a wilderness.[xxiv] As Christians, we understand that this world is not our home. We are on a journey to a promised land. That land is not the here and now. But God provides for us while we are on our wilderness journey. Like the Israelites and Jesus, we face many trials and temptations. At the top of the list are temptations regarding material wealth. Our consumer-driven economy tells us "get all you can get" for tomorrow is uncertain. We are asked to hoard material blessings so when times of trial come such as stock market crashes, unexpected illness, hospital bills, college tuition payments, etc., we will have "security." To be clear, it is certainly not sinful to earn honest wages or to save money for the future (whatever it may hold). Instead, the temptation is twofold: 1) trust ourselves to provide, and 2) trust the material wealth we accumulate. God gives us the ability to earn wages but he has also taught us that those wages are not to be trusted. After all, he has designed them to rot away. We must trust

[xxiii] Cunningham, 78.
[xxiv] Enns, 339.

God to provide for our needs not our greeds.[xxv] He gives us true bread that brings eternal life. However, this is not material bread but rather a relationship with Jesus Christ, the true bread of life. *"Store up treasures in heaven where moth and rust do not destroy"* (Matt. 6:20). You cannot trust material wealth because God designs it to rot away. *Trust the Provider not the provision.* God's provisions come with the responsibility to distribute them to others as they have need.

Bibliography

Black, Mark. *Luke.* The College Press NIV Commentary. Joplin, Mo.: College Press Publishing Company. 1996.

Blomberg, Craig. *Neither Poverty Nor Riches.* Grand Rapids: Eerdmans. 1999.

Burge, Gary. *John.* The NIV Application Commentary. Grand Rapids: Zondervan. 2000.

Carson, D. A. *The Gospel According to John.* The Pillar New Testament Commentary.Grand Rapids: Eerdmans. 1991.

Craigie, Peter. *The Book of Deuteronomy.* The New International Commentary on the Old Testament. Grand Rapids: Eerdmans. 1976.

Cunningham, Richard, *Creative Stewardship.* Nashville: Abingdon. 1979.

[xxv] Craig Blomberg, *Neither Poverty Nor Riches,* (Grand Rapids: Eerdmans, 1999), 131.

Enns, Peter. *Exodus.* The NIV Application Commentary. Grand Rapids: Zondervan. 2000.

Evans, C. F. *St. Luke.* The Trinity Press International New Testament Commentaries.Philadelphia: Trinity Press International. 1990.

Keener, Craig. *A Commentary on the Gospel of Matthew.* Grand Rapids: Eerdmans. 1999.

Lea, Thomas, and Hayne Griffin. *1, 2 Timothy & Titus.* The New American Commentary, Vol. 34. Nashville: Broadman. 1992.

Morris, Leon. *The Gospel According to St. Luke.* Tyndale New Testament Commentaries. Grand Rapids: Eerdmans. 1979.

Moss, C. Michael. *1, 2 Timothy & Titus.* The College Press NIV Commentary.Joplin, Mo.: College Press Publishing Company. 1994.

Nolland, John. *Luke 1-9:20.* Word Biblical Commentary. Dallas: Word Books. 1989.

Ridderbos, Herman. *The Gospel of John.* Grand Rapids: Eerdmans. 1997.

Sarna, Nahum. *Exodus.* The Jewish Publication Society Torah Commentary.Philadelphia: The Jewish Publication Society. 1991.

Chapter 11

CHRISTIAN STEWARDSHIP:

"A MAN'S LIFE DOES NOT CONSIST IN THE ABUNDANCE OF HIS POSSESSIONS" ~LUKE 12:15

by
Robert Horst, Entrepreneur

"The Earth is the Lord's and the fullness thereof." *Ps 24-1* You've heard this many times before, but do you really believe it? Does it apply to your life? If so, how? Do you truly believe that everything is the Lord's? If you do, how does it affect your day-to-day life? Good stewardship flows from following the knowledge that everything really does belong to God. That means the car you drive, the house you own or rent, your favorite CD, and everything else, including your bank account.

Have you noticed that God's instructions are always for our own good. They not only teach us about eternal truths, but they also make life on earth more pleasant. Take the ten commandments, for example. We have a happier life if we don't covet another's wife, house, or car. We can trust people if we know they don't lie, and life is a lot better if we're not going off murdering people. Can you imagine living in a world where these commandments were not seen as being valid? The ten commandments may make sense, but how can it possibly be good for us to believe and act as if everything really does belong to God? Let's consider the alternative.

If it were not true that everything belonged to God, then you would be able to claim ownership of some, or all things in your possession. Think about that. How might you justify that claim? You might start with "well, I paid for it with my own money," or "I received it from my Mother," or some other method of transfer of an asset to your control. Let's go back one step; where did you, (or your mother) get the money to purchase this?

You may reply "by working long, hard hours." Or, "by applying my skills to a certain task." Let's go back a second step: Where did those hours come from? Who provided the skills you have? Do you have control of time? Did you provide your skills? You may reply, "but I studied hard to learn those skills," or, "I put aside time to do this specific task." Again I would ask, who gave you the intellect to learn those skills, or whose time was it that you put aside. Did you create the minutes and hours you used?

The further back you try to go, the more you see that God is right (what a surprise!)... at bottom, everything is His. He provides the intellect to learn skills. He gives us the time to invest in our work. He gives us our daily bread. While it is true that if we are to achieve goals, we must apply effort, intellect and time, when we think about it, God is the ultimate source of all of those things. We simply use the gifts that He gave us. Of course, how we use these gifts is up to us.

Now back to the question, "How can it be good for me to believe and act as if everything really is God's?" Good stewardship flows directly from this concept. And wise choices that fulfill our lives and bring us joy flow directly from good stewardship. Again, let's consider the alternative. You are probably familiar with someone who purchases 'things' in order to achieve happiness.

Indeed, half of the ads on TV (those that don't push some message that asks you to 'see your doctor') promise that their product will make us happy. A new car will make you happy. A watch will make your wife or girlfriend happy. Diamonds make everyone happy. Do you really believe this? Are you willing to accept the lie that advertisers are really looking out for your happiness? I hope you are wiser than that. Do you see that true joy, as contrasted to momentary happiness, comes from an entirely different source? Talk to someone who has bought the car, the watch or the diamond, and see for yourself if it brought them happiness, much less real joy. Most likely you'll find that the person who was happy was the car dealer, the jeweler, or the sales rep. And they'll only be truly happy if they see that the money they just received belongs to God.

So... if we can see that material things won't bring us joy, where can we look for this joy? By following God's guidance. God really does want us to be joyful. He tells us this time and time again. And you receive true joy from following His guidance. In teaching His disciples, Jesus told them that he wanted them to have complete joy. John 15:11, and this would be achieved if they followed His commandments. In particular, we were commanded to "love one another."

By seeing that your money belongs to Him, you are unlikely to purchase some bauble, but rather are likely to see that you can use that money (His money, that is presently in your control) for a better purpose. By so doing, you avoid the trap of falling for the materialistic lie, and avoid the disappointment that will surely follow. And you have more resources to share with others.

This is the essence of good stewardship: By recognizing that God not only gives us these gifts, but He gives us guidance on how we are to use them. Jesus taught that the two guiding rules for living are: *Love your God, and love your neighbor. Matthew. 22:39* If we follow these rules, we are assured joy. And following these rules leads us to good stewardship.

"But", you may say, "that sounds all well and good, but what about the practical aspects of my life? How do I implement this concept as I go about my life?" By looking at four different gifts God gives us, we can begin to see the wisdom of God's guidance. Let's look at His gift of time, His gift of talents, His gift of natural resources, and His gift of money.

TIME: The Bible says we will enjoy life on this earth for a very short time: we're like a vapor, like the grass that withers. The time we have here should be used wisely. In addition to helping others, how can we use our time wisely?

TALENTS: God has given each of us unique and wonderful talents. The way we use these gifts speaks volumes about what we really believe. Let us not be guilty of burying our talents (Matthew 25: 15,ff)

NATURAL RESOURCES: The earth is the Lord's, and all that is in it. How do we treat God's creation? Do we abuse it, trash it, and think only of ourselves for the short run, or do we respect it, and consider others in our actions?

MONEY: It has been said, "would someone who looked at your checkbook know you were a Christian?" The way in which we handle our money is another strong indicator of our true beliefs.

One of the greatest benefits we reap as good stewards is the joy we get when we are able to give time, talents and money to others. The joys of good stewardship can only be received when start where Christ told us to start: Love God, and love one another. If we truly love God, we will respect the gifts He has given us. If we truly love one another, we will see their needs from an eternal, as well as temporal perspective.

To a very large extent, stewardship is about perspective. When Christ provided rules for living He was speaking in both the temporal, as well as eternal perspective. If we learn to see our lives, and resources (time, talents, money, resources) as gifts from God, to be used to bring glory to Him, we automatically become good stewards, and begin to reap the benefits that come from good stewardship. One way of looking at all of this is to see each of the gifts God has given us as gifts with limits on them. We have limited time, limited money, limited talents, and control limited resources. How we use these limited gifts says a lot about our real beliefs.

Lets look at these four aspects of stewardship in a bit more detail.

TIME:

Of all the resources God gives us, time is the most perplexing. We know our days are numbered, yet we often act as if our time will last forever. We know we should use every moment wisely, yet we often squander our time on things that don't matter. Sometimes we wonder how much time we have left, yet if we knew the answer, I wonder if it would make any difference? Or if we would even be glad we had that knowledge? Sometimes it takes a life-threatening event to cause us to see time in a new light, and to treat it as the very limited resource it is. One such event occurred in Bob's life. It changed his life. (Note: The examples used in this chapter represent real people, known to the author. Some names have been changed, but no circumstances have been altered or exaggerated to "prove" a point.

Bob had had a successful career, and was looking forward to early retirement, when he was diagnosed with an illness that could easily have ended his life in just a few months. Over the course of surgery, intensive care and recovery, Bob developed a new awareness of his mortality and how quickly life might end. "I had lost several good friends to cancer over the last five years" he said, "but somehow, the thought of me dying soon never really penetrated my consciousness. I saw how quickly life can change from being 'ordinary' to 'almost over'. I thought about what I had accomplished with the gifts God had given me, and I was unhappy with what I saw."

Realizing at a deep level that our time on earth is limited, and knowing that we are called to love our neighbor, we see that we must use our time to share God's love.

Jesus taught that we should invest our time in heavenly pursuits. Yet, while we are healthy and living a 'normal' life, we may find it difficult to pursue anything but the next day. Sometimes a life-changing event can be good for us.

Take this challenge: Pray daily that you will see the limits on your remaining time on earth, and that you will use your remaining days wisely. In three weeks, write yourself a note about how your perspective has changed, and how you are now using your time more wisely.

GIFTS AND TALENTS:

Dick was a successful executive. He managed a major company and was instrumental in the growth of his company over more than three decades. He managed a staff of hundreds and made sound decisions that helped guide his company, employees and customers. Throughout his career, he followed God's guidance in running his personal life, as well as his company. He gave generously to his church, supported missionaries across the world, and helped to lead a bible study for business executives. After retirement, he looked around for other ways he could help, and saw a real need in the inner city of Chester, PA. Dick offered his services to World Impact, and expected that they would appreciate his management skills and years of business experience. Instead, the most pressing need was for help in teaching inner city children, in this case, in the fourth grade. Instead of making executive decisions, Dick found himself as a teachers aide, helping little children learn. Dick says this is the most joy he has had in many years, and his joy was multiplied by the children and teachers. He was surprised to learn that God could use his talents in so many ways.

God has given each of us unique gifts and talents. Some people use them for their own gain, and some use them for others. Barry has a wonderful way with people, and could use those skills in a successful career in sales. Instead, he focuses on helping inner-city youth. In lieu of a huge paycheck and a nice house, he receives love from poor children, respect from those who appreciate what he is doing, and blessings that are impossible to count. When he talks about the children he is helping, he says "I receive the best reward anyone could ask for! I see kids who are growing up in the Lord, families who are increasing in love towards one-another and the Lord, and I praise God for the opportunity to do this."

Erin is blessed with great teaching skills. With a good education and seven years experience, she could teach anywhere she wanted. Instead of teaching in a wealthy school district, where she would be paid relatively well, and have students who had stable homes, she has chosen to work with the poorest of the poor. Instead of a big salary, Erin receives blessings of another sort. "I love to see 'my' kids scoring higher than wealthy suburban kids on their standardized tests" she says. "It proves these children can do anything they want, if they only have the support to lift them up. I'm so grateful to be able to be in a position to help them." She also has a wonderful opportunity to reflect Christ's love to her students and their families.

Rather than a good income measured in dollars, Erin receives blessings that are greater than any paycheck. While her dollar income is limited, she's never been hungry. She drives a ten year old car, but it gets her where she needs to go, and although her home is not in the best neighborhood, she and her husband are quite content. They take an eternal perspective, and it fills them with joy.

Wilma, although 88 years old, gets great joy of making 'lap robes' for what she calls the 'old folks' at a home near where she lives. She enjoys making the robes, but gets the greatest joy in giving the robes to people who wouldn't be able to make their own. Although she lives on a modest income of social security and a small pension, and has little money to give, she gives generously of her time.

In each case, these people have reaped tremendous rewards serving others rather than themselves. When Christ taught that we would gain treasure in heaven, he didn't imply that our treasure would be bestowed on us only when we got there. Each of the above examples shows that by being generous with our time and talents, we can enjoy greater blessings on earth, long before we join Christ in heaven. God has given us many gifts in terms of our talents and skills. If we recognize these as being 'from God' we are more likely to use them 'for God.'

Take this challenge: Think of two or three of your greatest gifts, and look around to see how you might help others with this talent. If you have trouble coming up with someone or an organization who might benefit from your talents, ask your pastor for suggestions. While you are at it, pray for that person or organization. At the end of three weeks, write a note to yourself, describing how you have been blessed by the giving.

RESOURCES

Another facet of stewardship is the way we treat God's creation. We are called to be stewards of the earth, and to appreciate and respect God's handiwork. Just as many people view money as 'theirs', not God's, some people view God's creation and creatures as something they have the right to destroy in the name of 'progress'. The connection between treating God's creation with respect and loving their neighbor is sometimes missed.

"Everyone is upstream from someone, and downstream from others." Anon. Loving your neighbor sometimes entails looking 'downstream' to see how your actions are affecting others. Sometimes those 'neighbors' can be many miles away.

When you look at natural beauty such as the Grand Canyon, or the stars in the sky, do you see God's handiwork? When you visit the shore, or a lake, do you see a beautiful present 'on loan' from God? If we really believe that we are to love our neighbor, then it is automatic that we will care for the blessings God has given us in a way that helps, not hurts, others. Recently, there have been a number of 'What would Jesus....'' the last word varies from "do", to "say", and even to 'drive'.

Asking "what would Jesus drive?" puts an interesting perspective on our use of resources. Would Jesus drive a car that got 18 miles to the gallon, knowing that he is helping to drive up energy costs, and make heating a home more difficult for the poor? Would he drive more often than is absolutely necessary, knowing that he is using up a limited resource that others need, and polluting the planet in the process? Would Jesus pour poisons or fertilizer on his lawn, knowing that they will wash downstream and poison fish that some people eat? Would Jesus waste electricity, knowing that his use of excess power contributes to climate change that hurts people in many lands? As in all of the lessons Christ provided, we can improve the way we live while on earth, if we show love for others. As always, His guidance applies to both temporal, as well as eternal life. For example: People who spend too much time driving, and don't get enough exercise, are at risk for a wide range of illnesses, from heart problems to diabetes, and obesity.

Joe had several health problems and a budget problem. He drove his car the six miles to his office and back each day. He had high blood pressure, high cholesterol and was 'pre-diabetic'. He was spending too much money on his car. When he decided to ride his bicycle to work, he began to improve his medical condition, while dramatically reducing the amount of carbon fuel he burned. Another benefit came from saving money on gasoline and having more money to give to his church, or support his family.

Christine, like most of us, didn't pay much attention to her use of electricity. She and her family used more than 1000 kilowatts each month, but didn't consider any alternatives until her local utility raised her rates by more than 19% in one year. After receiving her second bill of more than $250.00, she decided it was time to do something.

For a small investment, she replaced all of her light bulbs with compact florescent and the newer LEDs, wherever possible. The LED lights reduced her electric consumption by about 90% as compared to the old style bulbs she replaced, while the florescent reduced energy use by about 60%. Then, she challenged her family to be careful in their use of electricity. Turning off lights, limiting the use of hot water, keeping the air conditioning one degree warmer, and the heat one degree cooler all added up to big savings. Christine found that she could save more than $6.00 per month for each ceiling fan she didn't leave on all the time. After one winter month, she had dropped her electric bill significantly, had more money to spend on important things, and had reduced overall energy consumption. All of this, without enduring any real sacrifice.

In these examples, people who see how their actions affect others on the planet, and reduce consumption of resources, end up improving their lives, while helping others. They have more money to spend because they spent less on fuel, electricity, or other energy and they leave more resources for others. By limiting their demand for resources, they even help to keep costs down for others. By recognizing that all of us on earth are connected we show respect for God's creation and love for others as well.

Take this challenge: Think of ways your actions affect someone in another part of your state, another part of the country, and another part of the world. For example by reducing electric usage, you reduce air pollution in your local area, reduce the need for additional generating facilities and help to reduce the generation of more carbon dioxide into the atmosphere. Can you see similar examples in the food you eat, the clothes you wear, the house you live in?

MONEY

"God will reward your generosity many times over. Just send your check to us, and you will receive more wealth than you can imagine". - televangelist

"If I give all I have to the poor,... but have not love, I am nothing." 1 Corinthians. 13:3

"Money is the root off all evil". misquote (which is often used)

"He who has the most toys when he dies wins" *bumper sticker*

It is better to give than to receive.... how many of us have heard the Televangelists say that we should give money to their ministry because we will be rewarded with even more wealth if we do so? Of course, the logic of this approach fails the minute we realize that if that were true, they'd be giving money away, not collecting it! While rewards do most certainly follow the right kind of giving, it's not the gift that matters, so much as the reason the gift is given, and the heart with which it is done. St. Paul said that love is the most important aspect of our giving. Just as in all our other resources, if we focus on how money can be used in a loving manner to help others and move the church forward, we will be good stewards.

It isn't **money** that is the root of all evil. Money can do wonderful things when it is used as a tool to accomplish God's work. But the **love of money** is a terrible trap that is easy to fall into.

John grew up in a modest home in a modest neighborhood outside of Boston. After college, he held a number of modest jobs. He considered himself a 'good Catholic' and a religious person.

After several years of working for others, John determined he would start his own business. Over the years, success after success came his way, and his income climbed dramatically. After a few years, he made plans to move away from his modest neighborhood to one more in line with his new fortune. He bought a beautiful house on Cape Cod, a Mercedes for him, and another for his wife. He accumulated millions of dollars in investments.

Far from being happy in his new life, John became more and more focused on how much money he could accumulate. Every relationship became a contest to determine how much money John could squeeze from it. Every decision came to be made on the basis of how much money John could earn. Every aspect of his life became absorbed with money.

When I asked John how much money he could possibly need, his answer was "More". He wasn't just quoting a Robber Baron, and he wasn't being cute. He was being honest. He had accumulated more than 100 million dollars, but it wasn't enough. What he could not be made to see was that it was never enough, and unless he changed his heart, it could never be enough. He had come to worship money in the belief that it held some sort of security or made him better than others. John, it must be noted was a miserable and profoundly unhappy person. When you meet him, the first comparison one thinks of is that of Scrooge in "A Christmas Carol".

Carl had a similar background to John. He also became involved in a private business. As business increased, Carl also began to receive significant wealth. Unlike John, however, Carl saw this income as a tool to accomplish things; to improve the lives of his relatives; to give to organizations that could make a difference. As his wealth grew, Carl increased his giving until he was giving away almost 90% of his after-tax income.

John looked at Carl's giving as a sign of weakness, or guilt. One day, when I raised the subject to John, he declared that he wasn't feeling guilty about his assets or income, and saw no reason to try to assuage his guilt by giving money away. "Only fools", he went on, "give money away".

Ps. 37:21 "...The righteous give generously"

Which of these two persons are happier? John, who can't possibly get enough, no matter how much he may have, or Carl, who gives most of his income away? Needless to say, Carl is happier.

There are two major points here: John, who is in questionable health, cannot even realize that he 'can't take it with him', and can only think of adding to his wealth. In fact, he appears to have no control over his addiction to accumulate more and more wealth, even though he takes no joy in the process. He worries about leaving such an estate to his children, but can't consider any alternative. He doesn't realize that "his' money, which he feels he 'earned' by his hard work, is not really his. The very talents that have allowed him to earn all this money were gifts from God. Yet he insists on taking full credit for his success, and hoarding the results. Unfortunately, even after taking credit for his success, he still has no joy in his life.

The second point is that wealth, even extraordinary wealth cannot, under any circumstances, buy joy. In fact, in this case, it has brought more misery than joy.

So why do most of us have such a hard time giving our money away? I believe there are three reasons:

1. We think of it as 'our' money, not God's.
2. We fall for the lie that money can buy us security, status, or happiness.
3. We can't really believe that giving actually brings joy to the giver.

How can we change this mind-set? Think about John and Carl. Carl has realized that whatever he receives it was a gift. He gets great joy when he gives money to someone who can truly benefit from it, and he realizes that if money is the standard that someone uses to determine whether he is 'worthy' or not, then that person is no real friend.

Carl provides financial support for both Barry and Erin!

If we can only see things from an eternal perspective, and see how short our lives are, then it becomes easier to hold onto God's assets with a looser grip. When we know deeply that our job on earth is to glorify God, then whatever status we may hope to achieve through accumulating 'toys' and money, become meaningless.

Take this challenge: Test the idea that what you have, and what you earn, are truly gifts from God, over which He has given you stewardship. Think about how you can best use His wealth, and then actually do something with it.

Good stewardship arises when we recognize that, while on earth, we are blessed with gifts and resources that are limited. We have limited time, money, talents and worldly resources, and we are instructed to use what we do have wisely. Bringing glory to God by our wise decisions is the test of a good steward.

Take This Stewardship Test:

Have you recently received joy in giving to someone?

Do you turn off the lights when you leave a room?

Do you look at the bank account as 'your' money, or God's?

Do you turn off your car engine if you will be at idle for more than 30 seconds?

Do you use water-smart landscaping to minimize the water you use?

Do you drive a car that gets at least 27 mpg on the road?

Do you minimize the use of chemicals on your landscaping, and around the house?

Do you minimize the use of fertilizer around your home?

Do you minimize the use of hot water by doing your wash in cold/cool/warm water? By taking shorter showers?

Do you use energy minimizing lighting, such as compact florescent, or LED lights?

Do you get to share in the joy of helping those less fortunate than you?

Do you use your time wisely?

Do you appreciate the gifts God has given you, in terms of time, talents, income, resources? Do you see these gifts as truly belonging to God?

Do you thank God for every day? For every circumstance?

Do you pick up after your dog?

Do you pay attention to what resources were involved in the creation of the goods you purchase?

Are you aware of the unseen costs of some of the resources we take for granted?

When considering investments, do you look into the affect your company has on the long-term health of the planet God has given us?

Can you tell how each of these questions relates to good stewardship?

From an accounting perspective:

Can you see how the matters discussed in this chapter affect our cash flow, assets, liabilities, and statement of income and expense? What assets show up on our statement that are not terribly important? What assets might show up if the statement measured 'true riches'?

What happens to our cash flow when we observe good stewardship practices? Does this change lead to changes in our assets?

Chapter 12

THE INTEGRATION OF FAITH, REASON AND JUSTICE

FACULTY GOALS AND OBJECTIVES

By
Dr. Jack E. Bower
Eastern University

Business Professors are sometimes confronted with questions like, "How can you be a Christian and teach business?" Unfortunately, students sometimes equate business enterprise with worldliness and the love of money. The truth is that in a business context **knowledge is power**. Therefore business education is about empowerment. Empowered to serve God and others by increasing ones capacity for service. Empowered to realize one's full potential by being challenged to think and respond in totally new ways. Our goal as Christian business faculty is that our graduates are empowered to know what is just, to make the right decisions and use this knowledge for good instead of evil.

A good place to begin a business class is with a reading from Luke 16:1-13. It is a parable about management of accounts receivable. The story ends with this line; *"So if you have not been trustworthy in handling worldly wealth, who will trust you with true riches?"* Jesus is very clear in saying that the proper management of worldly wealth is a prerequisite to being trusted with spiritual wealth. The study of business can make you a more trustworthy steward of God's gifts to each of us and of His universe, if you seek to serve Him.

"Teachers can teach much more than their subject matter and much more than styles of thinking. They teach ethics and values and purpose and determination even while they are also teaching Finance 101. Teaching is a total process. While the finance may be taught analytically, those other things are being taught at the same time by selectively reinforcing, punishing, ignoring, and encouraging students. For the learner, <u>everything</u> in the teacher-learner situation is part of the educational process. In the classroom, students learn from the passion as well as the analytic virtuosity of their professors. They listen to integrity as well as brilliance, to determination as well as content..." [1]

The primary goal of Christian business faculty is to mentor all of the students on their spiritual journey in a right relationship with God. Their task is to encourage spiritual formation within the

---

[1] Leavitt, Harold J., <u>Corporate Pathfinders</u>, pp 96-97 (from faculty handbook).

church and academic community. Christian faculty will take the time to listen to the heart of each student and to make the time together a nurturing relationship.[2] Dr. Modica, the chaplain at Eastern University, calls this a transformational relationship instead of a transactional one. Faculty try to be critical without being cynical.[3] Christian faculty will try to convey a message of hope even if you are failing in a course.[4] Each professor struggles every day to search for that teachable moment when your heart is open to hearing the truth. May God give each of us, teachers and students alike, the wisdom, humility and courage to be in nurturing relationships.

The secondary goal of Christian business faculty is to help you integrate your faith into your professional and personal life.[5] For business students this means your faith must impact daily decision-making. Dr. Howard, a former Provost at Eastern University, describes life as a laboratory for testing our faith. He believes that there is no separation between the sacred and the secular,

[2] Pullias, Earl V., and others, Towards Excellence in College Teaching, (Dubuque: William C. Brown Co., 1963), page 35.

[3] Woodyard, David O., Beyond Cynicism, (Philadelphia: Westminster Press, MCMLXXII).

[4] Morris, William H., ed., Effective College Teaching, (Washington: American Council on Education, 1970), page 120.

[5] Ditmanson, Harold H., Howard V. Hong, and Warren A Quanbeck, eds., Christian Faith and the Liberal Arts, (Minneapolis: Augsburg Publishing House, 1960.), page 76.

Ferre, Nels F. S. Christian Faith and Higher Education, (New York: Harper & Brothers, 1954), page 28 on practical and professional capacities.

work is in fact worship.[6] The Business faculty wholeheartedly agrees with and practice this perspective.

Our total lives should be given to the glory of God. This means integrating our Christian values into the corporate environment where competition often demands taking a hard line.[7] Today, more than ever, Christian business educators need to train and graduate students who are not only competent in business skills but who also have a strong conscience.[8] Love your neighbor as yourself is a universal principle. Helping you to develop a strong conscience for right decision making is one of our most challenging tasks. We must continue to force you to think about complex justice issues.[9] Decisions made in the classroom over cases on ethics can have a significant impact on the real situations faced daily in life.[10]

Integration of faith and learning means that you will walk with God and show love toward others as outlined briefly in the above paragraphs.[11] These are,

[6] The speech was given on 4/21/96 to the graduate student worship assembly. This speech by Dr. Howard and our conversation afterwards had a major influence on the outline of this paper.

[7] Holloway, Richard, Crossfire: Faith and Doubt in an Age of Certainty, (Grand Rapids: William E. Eerdmans Publishing Co., 1988), page 36.

[8] Phenix, Philip H., Education and the Worship of God, (Philadelphia: Westminster Press, MCMLXVI), page 115.

[9] Pelikan, Jaroslav J., and others, Religion and the University, (Canada: University of Toronto Press, 1964), page 121.

[10] McKeachie, Wilbert J., New Directions for Teaching and Learning, (San Francisco: Jossey-Bass Inc. 1980), page 44, "Learning from Prototype Models."

[11] Bondi, Robert C., To Love as God Loves, (Philadelphia: Fortress Press, 1987), page 20.

in fact, the greatest of the commandments (Matt. 22:37-40). Professors like to reason from the general to the specific. The following are five specific business objectives (Christ like perspectives) that we try to instill in all of our students. The ordering is not significant because the needs are different for each student:

#1 EXPERIENCE LIFE, BE A RISK TAKER: My parents were fond of saying that people who never make any mistakes are people who never do anything. *"Experience is the school of life. We are not confronted with clear propositions to be accepted or rejected, but with complicated situations within which we must learn."*[12] Doing something is usually better than doing nothing; perfectionism can lead to procrastination or inactivity.[13]

We operate in an extremely complex economy. Students often need help in breaking down complex tasks into steps that can be accomplished one at a time. Accounting and finance professors, for example, focused their teaching energies on making the complex financial world understandable and entertaining to students.[14] Dr. Campolo is fond of saying that *education is entertainment with a purpose.*

Risk taking, one step at a time, is a valuable lesson for success in the business world. Even in the spiritual world we need to be risk takers. Jesus said, *"Whoever finds his life will lose it, and whoever loses his life for my sake will find it"*(Matt. 10:39). Whether in following

[12] Ferre, Nels F.S., Christian Faith and Higher Education, (New York: Harper & Brothers, 1954), page 78.
[13] Phillips, J.B., Your God is too Small, (The MacMillan Company-New York), page 28.
[14] Fowler, James W., Becoming Adult, Becoming Christian, (San Francisco: Harper & Row, 1984), page 95.

Jesus or in business decision-making, we all need to take risks. We have only to study the heroes of the Bible to see risk takers, from the Patriarch to Jesus. Great things were accomplished by risk takers acting one step at a time. Jesus told a parable about a wealthy landowner who gave management of his vineyard to a certain group of evil managers. The landowner sent auditors to the vineyard who were ignored or mistreated. In the end, he sent his son who was killed. Jesus was a risk taker in coming to earth to die for our sins.[15] The servant who had the one mina *"laid it away in a piece of cloth"* was rebuked by Jesus for not taking the risk of investing the money with the moneychangers. When David heard Goliath boasting, he said, why not send me. Some of the most successful entrepreneurs are so because they are risk takers.

Risk taking is of particular interest when teaching finance where the class spends a considerable amount of time on financial markets and risk. In this setting, you are encouraged to dream and contemplate the risks and rewards of financial management. Walking with God also has its risks and rewards. Certainly you need to see people in various walks of life and say, why not me? I could do that someday!

Risk takers also know how to make a break with their past. Paul participated in the stoning of Stephen, yet he didn't let this keep him from looking towards the future. *"Forgetting what is behind and straining towards the goal to win the prize for which God has called me heavenward in Christ Jesus"* (Phil 3:13). You will be encouraged to strain toward the goal, to win the prize. Many people are afraid of the future; they back

---

[15] Philippians 2:6ff.

away from it and live in the past.[16] Christians should be straining forward ready for new challenges and new opportunities, "to take full advantage of this present; to live this day as if it were our last, as if we were going to die as martyrs at the end of the day."[17]

Risk takers are the salt and light spoken of in Matt. 5:13. In a recent newspaper comic strip, the punch line read like this, *"Yep life sure is a great gift, but I guess there's always going to be those content to play with just the box."*[18] I like the quote from Dr. Campolo; *"I try to help young people see them-selves as agents of God, commissioned to a vocation of ultimate importance. With this understanding, they'll have a sense of calling that generates unparalleled enthusiasm for life."*[19]

#2 HAVE A SENSE OF DESTINY AND A SENSE OF GOD'S PROTECTION: Jesus said, *"You have no power over me unless it was given to you from on high"* (John 19:11). Luke said, God has *"determined the times set for them and the exact places where they should live"* (Acts 17:26). You need to seek God's will for your life.[20] You need to know that if you are seeking Him, your next job or next project is a part of God's purpose for your life.[21] When faced with a tough decision we all need to remember to pray about it, asking God to reveal his

---

[16] Woodyard, David O., <u>Beyond Cynicism</u>, (Philadelphia: Westminster Press, MCMLXXII), page 55 "The Power of the Future."

[17] Galilea, Segundo, <u>Spirituality of Hope</u>, (Maryknoll: Orbis Books, 1978), page 62.

[18] Phila. Inquirer, <u>Bent Halos</u>.

[19] MacTavish, Stephanie, <u>A Joyful Community, Living the Life of Faith at Eastern College</u>, 1996.

[20] Romans 8:12ff.

[21] Roberts, Oral., <u>Miracle of Seed-Faith</u>, (Tulsa: Fleming H Revell Co., 1970).

---

will to us so that we choose the correct path.[22] You will find that the business faculty believe that God has a plan for their lives and that in being at Eastern University they are doing what He has called them to do.[23] You should learn to feel a sense of destiny in your professional as well as personal life.[24]

Destiny, like most spiritual gifts, is a magnet that pulls us closer to God.[25] The hard part is knowing when opposition to our plans is God trying to show us another road or is He testing us.[26] We certainly don't want to ignore God's messages. Giving Him the credit in every situation is a key to joyful living. So many people feel distant from God when problems enter their lives.[27] The truth is that these may be the moments when they could be the closest to God.[28] It can sometimes be very difficult to see the leading of God in

[22] Trueblood, Elton, A Place to Stand, (Harper & Row, Publishers, 1969), page 82, The Reality of Prayer. (I often mention this book in class when talking about net present value; NPV is the place to stand in finance just like the resurrection is the place to stand for Christians).

[23] Fisher, Fred, The Purpose of God and the Christian Life, (Westminster Press, Philadelphia, MCMLXII), page 113.

[24] I like the explanation of Calvinism often given by Dr. Miles. "When we get to heaven and walk through the arch it will say *for whosoever will*. When we have passed through the arch and look back, it will say *predestined from the foundations of the world.*

[25] James 1:2ff and II Corinthians 5:1ff.

[26] Jones, Laurie Beth, Jesus, CEO (Chief Executive Officer), (New York:Hyperion, 1995). This is a devotional book that I often use in my accounting class because of her keen insights into the leadership style of Jesus.

[27] Carey, George, "Archbishop of Canterbury", Why I Believe in a Personal God, (Harold Shaw Publishers, Wheaton, Il.), "Good, Evil and God", page 73.

[28] Kennedy, Eugene C., Believing, (Garden City: Doubleday & Company, 1974), page 64.

your life and to learn from an unpleasant experience.[29] Chapter 14 will explore this topic in more depth.

#3 SUBMIT TO AUTHORITIES: For business students paying taxes and obeying the laws of the government are major issues.[30] We all must learn to show respect to government officials as opposed to resenting their intrusions into our lives.[31] It is interesting to note that the early debates over the constitutionality of the income tax concerned the government knowing this type of personal information.[32] The function of government is to "prolong and protect" our precious moments here on earth.[33] If you major in accounting, you will spend a considerable amount of time discussing attitudes about paying taxes. We have clear direction from God to pay our taxes (Romans 13: 6ff) & (Matt. 22:15ff).[34] Unfortunately, the world creates a different expectation in the minds of students where profit comes from the victimization of other taxpayers.[35] Any

[29] Foster, Richard J., Prayer, (San Francisco: Harper Collins, 1964), page 23.

[30] Scharf, Betty R. The Sociological Study of Religion, (Harper Torchbooks, London, 1970). Dr. Scharf is a lecturer in Sociology in the London School of Economics. This text and others suggest that religion was created and is maintained by governments to keep its citizens in submission to authority.

[31] Romans 13:2ff.

[32] Hoffman, Smith, Willis, Individual Income Taxes, (West's Federal Taxation, 1996 edition, Eagan, MN), Chapter One.

[33] Lewis, C.S., Beyond Personality, (The MacMillian Co., N.Y., 1947), page 43.

[34] Newell, William R., Romans Verse by Verse, (Moody Press, Chicago, 1938).

[35] Borsch, Frederick Houk, God's Parable, (The Westminster Press, Phila, 1975), page 72, Acts of Power.

accountant who is a Christian can tell story upon story of people who seek to deceive the IRS on their tax returns including some Christian nonprofit organizations whom file Form 990, an information return. God does not favor those who practice rebellion and deceitfulness.[36]

On the other hand, this does not mean that we should not work to correct problems in our society not being addressed by the government or that we should not seek to change our government.[37] It is important to learn to be good citizens, to exercise your right to vote and to hold elected officials accountable for the decisions they make.[38] Some of the best discussions in class have followed chapel speeches by Christians immersed in the world's moral problems. These are critical issues for discussion and a part of the integration of faith reason and justice.

#4 AVOID BEING SEDUCED BY MATERIALISM: Satan says, "He who dies with the most toys wins!" Jesus says, "*A man's life does not consist in the abundance of his possessions*" (Luke 12:13-21). One of our great struggles as Christians is not to be seduced by the world into defining success in Satan's terms.[39] The world says it is what you do as a profession or your physical appearance that defines your self-worth. Christians should resent both of these perspectives. It

[36] Romans 13:2.
[37] Trueblood, D. Elton, The Marks of a Christian College, (Found in *Towards a Christian Philosophy of Higher Education,* John Paul von Grueningen Editor, The Westminster Press, Phila, MCMLVII), page 161.
[38] Ramm, Bernard, The Christian College in the Twentieth Century, (William B. Eerdmans Publishing Co. Grand Rapids, Michigan), page 64.
[39] Fowler, James W., and Sam Keen., Life Maps, (Waco: Word Books, 1978), page 109.

is our relationship to God through His Son that defines who we are. There is a self-confidence that comes from being a child of God. Mankind looks on the outside but God sees on the inside (Mark 2:8). Our goal is to have His eyes, to see the pure heart and Godlike qualities in everyone. Yet, at the same time we have to be trained to recognize evil and avoid it. Bringing a discussion about the love of money or preoccupation with acquiring wealth into the classroom can be difficult.[40] Students generally do not like to talk about it unless encouraged to do so.[41] The question "Is greed good" is a great beginning point. Sometimes student will say that they will never have enough money to be happy.

We have to create a sensitivity for the needy of this world as we grow in our love of God and neighbors.[42] You must see success in terms of the positive impact you have had on others and in terms of the people you have trained to carry on after you are gone. Like Paul, we should learn to be content whatever the circumstances. *"I know what it is to be content in any and every situation, whether well fed or hungry, whether living in plenty or in want. I can do everything through him who gives me strength"* (Phil 4:12,13).

#5 KEEP YOUR WORK IN THE PROPER PERSPECTIVE: We serve a working God. His work is great, awesome and marvelous. Because we are made in the image of God, we also should be creatures of work. Work

---

[40] Marstin, Ronald., <u>Beyond Our Tribal Gods</u>, "The Maturing of Faith", (Orbis Books, Maryknoll, N.Y. 1982), page 125, "Wealth and the Gospel".

[41] I have read several books on "Christian Financial Concepts" by Larry Burket and I often use his techniques in class. I have also taught workshops in churches using books and tapes published by his organization.

[42] Eastern College Mission Statement.

provides the income that buys food, clothing and shelter and the opportunities to share with others. God speaks out against laziness in II Thessalonians 3:6ff. *"And whatever you do, whether in word or deed, do it all in the name of the Lord Jesus Christ, giving thanks to God the Father through him"* (Col. 3:17).

There has been significant criticism of the "Protestant work ethic." Certainly when taken to extremes, work can be destructive. If too much time is given to the job and therefore family or the church community is neglected, it is a problem.[43] The Christian work ethic is not dead. You will be encouraged to perform intense and diligent work while in college and after graduation. Hopefully, you will have a balanced perspective so that you can make the proper choices between work and family.[44] "For God did not give us a spirit of timidity, but a spirit of power, of love and of self-discipline."[45]

The work issue is critical for accounting majors where many public accounting firms ask employees to work 60 hours per week during the tax and audit season. Release time is then given during the summer and fall. Phil Zink, a former accounting professor at Eastern University, liked to say that you cannot get sick, fall in love, or get married during tax season. The message from accounting alumni is always the same. Be prepared for long hours during the audit and tax season.

[43] Ferre, Nels F.S., Christian Faith and Higher Education, (New York: Harper & Brothers 1954), page 115

[44] Byrne, H.W., A Christian Approach to Education, (Zondervan Publishing House, Michigan, 1961), page 276. Dr. Byrne was Dean of Fort Worth Bible College. His book has an excellent list of learning objectives in many subject areas. The list for economics is well done.

[45] II Timothy 1:7.

SUMMARY

If we as Christian business faculty have motivated you to have the courage to take risks, have a sense of purpose, show the proper respect for authority, not to be lovers of money and know how to keep life's choices in perspective; then we have been successful in our endeavor as teachers.[46] While holding students in the highest regard, we truly want to call you to a Godly standard.[47] This is the integration of faith, reason and justice and is our purpose as faculty for being here at this place and time.

[46] This is not intended as an all inclusive list. There are excellent lists in a book by C. Robert Pace, <u>Education and Evangelism</u>, (Carnegie Commission on Higher Education, McGraw-Hill Book Co., N.Y., 1972).

[47] Ficken, Charence E. <u>Building a Faculty</u>, (Nashville: Board of Education of the Methodist Church, 1956), page 29.

Bibliography

Bondi, Roberta C. To Love as God Loves. Philadelphia: Fortress Press, 1987.

Borsch, Frederick H. God's Parable. Philadelphia: The Westminster Press, 1975.

Bowden, John, and James Richmond, ed. A Reader in Contemporary Theology. Philadelphia: The Westminster Press, 1967.

Bruce, F. F. The Tyndale New Testament Commentaries. Grand Rapids: William B. Eerdmans Publishing Company, 1969.

Byrne, H. W. A Cristian Approach to Education. Grand Rapids: Zondervan Publishing House, 1961.

Carey, George. Why I Believe in a Personal God. Wheaton: Harold Shaw Publishers, 1989.

Ditmanson, Harold H., Howard V. Hong, and Warren A. Quanbeck, eds. Christian Faith and the Liberal Arts. Minneapolis: Augsburg Publishing House, 1960.

Donceel, Joseph F. The Searching Mind. London: University of Notre Dame Press, 1979.

Ferre, Nels F. S. Christian Faith and Higher Education. New York: Harper & Brothers, 1954.

Ferre, Nels F. S. Reason in Religion. London: Thomas Nelson and Sons LTD, 1963.

Ficken, Clarence E. Building a Faculty. Nashville: Board of Education of The Methodist Church, 1956.

Fisher, Fred L. The Purpose of God and the Christian Life. Philadelphia: The Westminster Press, 1952.

Foster, Richard J. Prayer. San Francisco: Harper Collins, 1964.

Fowler, James W. Becoming Adult, Becoming Christian. San Francisco: Harper & Row, 1984.

Fowler, James W., and Sam Keen. Life Maps. Waco: Word Books, 1978.

Galilea, Segundo, trans. Spirituality of Hope. Maryknoll: Orbis Books, 1989.

Holloway, Richard. Crossfire: Faith and Doubt in an Age of Certainty. Grand Rapids: William B. Eerdmans Publishing Company, 1988.

Jones, Laurie Beth. Jesus, CEO. New York: Hyperion, 1995.

Kennedy, Eugene C. Believing. Garden City: Doubleday &Company, 1974.

LeFevre, Perry. The Christian Teacher. New York: Abingdon Press, MCMLVIII.

Lewis, C. S. Beyond Personality. New York: The Macmillan Company, 1947.

Mackenzie, Donald M., and Manning M. Pattillo. Church-Sponsored Higher Education in the United States. Washington: American Council on Education, 1966.

Marstin, Ronald. Beyond Our Tribal Gods. Maryknoll: Orbis Books, 1979.

McKeachie, Wilbert J. New Directions for Teaching and Learning. San Francisco: Jossey-Bass Inc., 1980

Morris, William H., ed. Effective College Teaching. Washington: American Council on Education, 1970.

Newbigin, Lesslie. Proper Confidence. Grand Rapids: William B. Eerdmans Publishing Company, 1995.

Newell, William R. Romans. Chicago: Moody Press, 1938.

Pace, C. Robert. Education and Evangelism. New York: McGraw-Hill Book Company, 1972.

Parsonage, Robert R., ed. Church Related Higher Education. Valley Forge: Judson Press, 1978.

Pelikan, Jaroslav J., and others. Religion and the University. Canada: University of Toronto Press, 1964.

Phenix, Philip H. Education and the Worship of God. Philadelphia: The Westminster Press, MCMLXVI.

Phillips, J. B. Your God is Too Small. New York: The MacMillan Company, 1958.

Pullia, Earl V., and others. Toward Excellence in College Teaching. Dubuque: William C. Brown Company, 1963.

Ramm, Bernard. The Christian College in the Twentieth Century. Grand Rapids: William B. Eerdmans Publishing Company, 1963.

Roberts, Oral. Miracle of Seed-Faith. Tulsa: Fleming H. Revell Company, 1970.

Robertson, Roland, ed. Sociology of Religion. Baltimore: Penguin Books, 1969.

Scharf, Betty R. The Sociological Study of Religion. New York: Harper & Row, 1970.

Schuller, Robert H. Tough Minded Faith for Tender Hearted People. Nashville: Thomas Nelson Publishers, 1983.

Thiessen, Elmer J. Teaching for Commitment. London: McGill-Queen's University Press, 1993.

Thomas, J. D. The Spirit and Spirituality. Abilene: Biblical Research Press, 1966.

Trueblood, Elton. A Place to Stand. New York: Harper & Row, 1969.

Von Grueningen, John Paul, ed. Toward a Christian Philosophy of Higher Education. Philadelphia: The Westminster Press, MCMLVII.

Woodyard, David O. Beyond Cynicism. Philadelphia: Westminster Press, MCMLXXII.

Chapter 13

DEVOTIONS IN ACCOUNTING:

INTEGRATION OF ACCOUNTING PRINCIPLES AND FAITH IN CHRIST JESUS

By
Dr. Jack E. Bower
Eastern University

INTEGRATION AS A GOAL

A major goal of your Christian professors is to promote spiritual formation within students. Spiritual training is one of the unique functions we offer as Christian faculty. Students tend to compartmentalize their thinking into a spiritual realm and a business realm and often have great difficulty integrating the two. In your business classes, we will use the Bible as a casebook of God's interaction with those who choose to follow Him. Through probing Bible stories from a business perspective, you will learn to integrate business and faith and so will develop your ability to think inclusively.

INTEGRATION DEFINED

Our task as Christian business faculty is to provide tools to help you see the entire world through a spiritual perspective. When we are successful, you will apply spiritual principles to the business world and, conversely, will understand scripture with help from business principles. Then you will be able to think inductively by contrasting and comparing problem situations. You will be able to identify common elements between biblical principles and business situations presented inside or outside the classroom. When you are able to do this, true integration is taking place.

PEDAGOGY

Our attempts at integration will occur both systematically and spontaneously throughout the limited time we have with you. Professors always are looking for that "teachable moment." Friendships between professors and students will develop inside and outside the classroom and often will continue beyond graduation. The most intense times of mentoring will occur during office hours, but certainly the classroom provides the most consistent time of interaction and of probing biblical principles. It is absolutely essential that you view the classroom as a safe environment in which to express opinions different from those of the professor. Sometimes it is more critical for the professor to understand what you are saying than to express an opinion or insight. Your professors pray regularly for the gift of being able to gently challenge your reasoning without threatening your feelings of safety in expression. Spiritual formation is impossible without the Holy Spirit working in both the teacher and the student.

The following devotions integrate principles of accounting with principles from God's Word. After setting the stage with a series of core theological values, the devotions follow the topical outline of a typical accounting book.

TEN CORE THEOLOGICAL QUESTIONS AND VALUES

1. IS YOUR ATTITUDE ABOUT MONEY A THEOLOGICAL ISSUE? DOES IT MATTER IN TERMS OF FINDING SALVATION? The answer is yes! *Read Matthew 19:16-26; Mark 10:17-27; or Luke 18:18-27.* This is commonly referred to as the story of the "Rich Young Man" who "went away sad, because he had great wealth" (New International Version). The point of the story: Wealth is a hindrance to following Jesus. Poverty will not necessarily save a person, and wealth will not necessarily condemn a person to hell. It is simply more difficult for the rich to follow Jesus than for the poor.

2. CAN RICHES CHOKE THE WORD OF GOD SO THAT IT PRODUCES NOTHING? Jesus loved to tell stories with heavenly meanings (parables). *Read Matthew 13:3-8, 18-23; Mark 4:3-8, 14-20; or Luke 8:5-8, 11-15.* Known as the "Parable of the Sower," the story teaches that God's Word is like seed sowed in the world. The seed sowed in thorns is like the person who hears the Word but is choked by the lure of riches and the worries of this world. Concern for one's wealth keeps the seed from growing and limits the person's ability to respond to the Good News. This truth is corroborated by the fact that the Gospel is often

more readily received and accepted in less financially affluent communities.

3. WHO DO YOU TRUST FOR SECURITY? From God's perspective, the answer to this question involves the concept of idolatry. (To "idolize" means to feel excessive devotion for something or someone.) *Read Matthew 6:19-24.* Jesus said your heart will follow your treasure. The world teaches us to trust in our wealth for security. Wall Street and Hollywood have become holy ground for the idolatry of wealth and power. Should you save for your retirement? Yes, because our culture does not place the burden of elder care upon the children. But the real issue is who—or what—you really trust to take care of you: your pension plan or God.

4. IS GREED GOOD? One of the finance Web sites runs a column called "Greed Is Good." Greed means never having enough—never enough cars, homes, share of corporate ownership, bonds, and so on. It is never enough. *Read Luke 12:13-21.* God did not call the man who hoarded his possessions wicked, but a fool. Jesus said the greedy are foolish. They are mistaken about life. Abundant life, according to God, does not arise from or necessitate an abundance of possessions.

5. HOW IMPORTANT ARE GENEROSITY AND REPAYING WRONGS? In many cultures a tax collector or tax-forms preparer negotiates the tax owed with an individual taxpayer and then negotiates for a lesser amount from the taxing authority. The difference belongs to the tax preparer as fees

earned. Rome used such a system in the time of Jesus, and the Italian government today uses a similar system. A senior tax collector, Zacchaeus, operating under such a system is featured in one Bible story. *Read Luke 19:1-10.* Zacchaeus' response to Jesus' message was one of extreme generosity. He gave half of his possessions to the poor and repaid those whom he had cheated an amount worth four times what he'd taken from them! In the words of Jesus, "Today salvation has come to this house" (NIV). Certainly poverty does not mean moral purity, and wealth does not bar salvation. But in this story, Zacchaeus traded his wealth for salvation. He was a much different tax collector after his encounter with Jesus.

6. HOW IMPORTANT IS EQUAL TREATMENT OF THE WEALTHY AND THE POOR? *Read James 2:1-9.* James condemned those who made class distinctions in the church. Who are the leaders of the church today? Do we elect or appoint into leadership positions the poor or the rich? We tend to equate success in the business world and success in the spiritual world, but basing decisions about leadership positions on a person's wealth are wrong. According to James, "God has chosen those who are poor in the eyes of the world to be rich in faith" (NIV).

7. HOW CRITICAL IS ECONOMIC JUSTICE TO SALVATION? *Read James 5:1-6.* James harshly condemned the wealthy for not paying a fair wage, and he also condemned an unjust distribution system. This passage also establishes the "Rust

Principle": If you have possessions that are idle and rusting away such as an old car or boat or motorcycle, you have too many possessions. Ownership carries responsibility. You need to get rid of assets you do not use. Jesus said, "Go, sell your possessions and give to the poor" (Matthew 19:21, NIV).

8. IN THE NEW TESTAMENT, WHAT WAS THE GOAL OF GIVING TO THE CHURCH? Sharing resources was a central characteristic of the early church. *Read Acts 2:44-47.* What are our goals today in giving to the church? Examine your church budget and see how much is allocated toward serving the poor. For example, what is your church doing to meet the needs of the homeless?

9. DOES WEALTH CONFLICT WITH THE SPIRITUAL NATURE OF THE KINGDOM? The Old Testament details God's *physical* blessings upon those who follow Him, and the Kingdom had a physical presence in the nation of Israel and in God's Holy Temple. Did Jesus make a fundamental paradigm shift in the Kingdom of God from the physical to the spiritual? *Read John 18:36-37.* The *spiritual* Kingdom promised by Jesus does not promise physical wealth as a sign of God's blessings, nor is wealth considered evil (for example, the streets of heaven are described as being of pure gold). There is also no command to repudiate the wealth of the physical world. We are to live in the world but not become seduced by it (James 4:4; Luke 9:25).

10. IT IS IMPOSSIBLE TO PROVIDE FOR THE PHYSICAL
    NEEDS OF OTHERS UNLESS YOU POSSESS SOME
    RESOURCES OF YOUR OWN? Do you ever feel a
    sense of inconsistency in the passages that deal
    with wealth? *Read Hebrews 13:2 and Matthew
    6:19.* We are commanded to be hospitable, but
    hospitality takes resources. Is it easier for the
    person with an extra bed to entertain the
    stranger? How much to own and how much to
    give away is a constant dilemma for North
    American Christians. The critical issue,
    according to Paul in 1 Timothy 6:17, is *hope.* Do
    we place our "hope in God" or our "hope in
    wealth, which is so uncertain" (NIV)?

DOUBLE-ENTRY ACCOUNTING

What is the origin of double-entry accounting? Was
modern accounting divinely inspired? Two professions,
accounting and law, maintain justice and social order.
Our God is a God of justice. *Read James 5:4-5.* How do
you know what you owe the laborers without an
accounting system? How do you know what is a just
profit unless you record revenue and all expenses (the
matching principle)? As trading partnerships
developed in the 1200s, the church had a great concern
over the calculation of a just profit. The timing was
perfect; the great theologian St. Thomas Aquinas had
both the opportunity and the motive to develop the
accounting system we have today.[1]

---

[1] ACCOUNTING'S SAINTLY ANCESTRY: The possible
    Influence of Saint Thomas Aquinas on the
    Development of Double Entry Accounting, <u>Accounting
    Through the Eyes of Faith,</u> 2nd edition, compiled by
    Jack E. Bower, 2002.

DEBITS AND CREDITS

The most famous credit in the Bible was the faith of Abraham (Genesis 15:6). *Read Romans 4:1-8.* Paul quotes the reference to Abraham's credit seven times in the New Testament. The business term "credit" actually came from the Greek translation of the Bible known as the Septuagint. Paul was raised as a Greek and would have studied the Septuagint. In God's accounting equation, we are an accounts receivable while credits decrease our debit balance. The term credit also is used in Romans 4:4 when referring to the increase in wages payable. Can our human credits save us? Said another way, can we earn our salvation? The answer is no. Only the blood of Jesus Christ frees us from sin and death.

MEASUREMENT ISSUES

What does accounting measure? Not all financial transactions are measured by the accounting system. Signing contracts or determining prices significantly impacts the organization's finances, but these actions are not recorded in the accounting system. An organization's most important asset usually is its human capital, which also is not recorded in the accounting system. What does God's spiritual accounting system measure? Actions, yes, but also motives. *Read Matthew 5:27-29, 43-48.* We are called to have pure thoughts and pure hearts with unbounded love for our enemies. God sees our actions, knows our hearts, and judges our motives.

THE ENTITY CONCEPT

The concept of "Separate Entity" is critical to the ability of the accounting equation to properly record transactions and measure performance. What type of entity is God? What type of entity is our spiritual life? *Read John 10:24-38.* The "God Head" acts like a partnership. The relationship between the Father, Son, and Holy Spirit is one of mutual agency. We, on the other hand, are more like a publicly held corporation that requires outside investments to grow spiritually. We receive investments from parents, friends, and from the Holy Spirit at work within our lives.

THE ACCOUNTING EQUATION

If God needed to keep accounting records and used the accounting equation, what would the equation look like? The assets would include all of heaven and earth. Inventory would have included mankind before the fall. After the fall, we became accounts receivable to God. Each of our sins increases our accounts receivable on God's books as well as an increase to His liability account called sin. A God of justice must punish sin. *Read Matthew 6:9-13 and Genesis 15:6.* The scriptures consistently equate sin with debt and equate faith as a credit against our accounts receivable held by God.[2]

GENERALLY ACCEPTED ACCOUNTING PRINCIPLES (GAAP)

How critical is trust in human relationships? In financial relationships between investors and corporations, trust is defined as Generally Accepted Accounting Principles (GAAP). Our relationship with God is also one of trustworthiness. *Read Luke 16:10-13.* Jesus calls us to be trustworthy in our handling of

[2] HEAVENLY ACCOUNTING: God's Accounting System Revealed Through the Scriptures, Accounting Through the Eyes of Faith, compiled by Jack E. Bower, Eastern College, 2000.

worldly wealth so that God can trust us with true spiritual riches.[3]

REVENUE RECOGNITION

When is revenue recognized? This question continually presents itself on the pages of the *Wall Street Journal* in a section called "Money and Investing." Corporations, analysts, and shareholders argue principles of revenue and expense recognition with the Securities and Exchange Commission (SEC)— and sometimes in the courts. Humans do the same thing with God. We suppress our conscience and rationalize away sin until we convince ourselves that God does not see or care about our little injustices or careless words. *Read Matthew 12:33-37.* Jesus says everything we say is recorded and that we will face our sins on the Day of Judgment.

MONEY MEASUREMENT

Accounting uses money as a unit of measure. If it cannot be expressed as money, is it recorded as a journal entry? The Old Testament gave the Jewish nation some specific measures of sin. Jesus shifted the paradigm and changed the unit of measure. *Read Matthew 5:13-16.* Our call as Christians is to be salt and light in a fallen world by changing the unit of measure. We ask others to consider following Jesus, making Him Lord of their lives, and then we ask them to see every transaction through a new spiritual lens.

---

[3] SCRIPTURAL ADMONITION TO STUDY ACCOUNTING, Accounting Through the Eyes of Faith, compiled by Jack E. Bower, Eastern College, 2000.

JOURNAL ENTRIES

High school and college students often are required to keep a written journal of their experiences as a method of learning through writing. Jesus commonly used stories to instruct, and the scriptures are a sort of journal of the Jewish nation, the life of Jesus Christ, and the history of the church. Luke, for example, provides the most orderly account of Jesus' life. In journalizing for a business, materiality is always an issue; only the material or significant events are recorded, requiring a great deal of judgment on the part of the accountant. The same issue of materiality faced the Gospel writers as they journalized the life of Jesus. *Read John 21:24-25.* In our spiritual lives, Jesus calls us to be accountable for the material issues of life. Every sin hurts God, but we tend to minimize our own sins and magnify the sins of others. Jesus said, "Why do you look at the speck of sawdust in your brother's eye and pay no attention to the plank in your own eye?" (Matthew 7:3, NIV). (This is a little Godly humor regarding our decisions to spiritually journalize what is material and what is not material.)

THE MATCHING PRINCIPLE

Periodicity and the matching principle attempt to provide for a trustworthy net income. Adjustments to the accounting records recognize revenue and expenses in the proper time period. It is an essential accounting principle for trustworthy earnings, but it does not work in terms of salvation. As humans, we have a tendency to match our good deeds against our bad deeds and then feel good about ourselves. Can a dedicated life of service to God guarantee salvation? The answer is no! Only through the blood of Jesus Christ can we find salvation. It is not earned, and it is certainly not a matter of doing more good deeds than bad deeds. *Read Ephesians 2:4-9.* Salvation is a gift from God, pure and simple.

CLOSING ENTRIES

Closing entries move or transfer the balances from the temporary accounts into the permanent accounts. For nonbelievers, their spiritual books will close when they face death and transition from the physical world to the spiritual world. All temporary accounts on this earth will be closed. *Read 1 John 3:11-20.* When we accept Jesus Christ as King of our lives, the books of our old lives are closed and we pass from death to life. The names of those who choose life are recorded in the "book of life." The Apostle John says in verse 17 that the evidence of this transfer from death to life is the way we address the needs of the poor with our material wealth.

TRIAL BALANCE

We are encouraged to evaluate our lives continually in light of the Word of God. This can happen in times of prayer, and it happens for many Christians during Communion. *Read 1 Corinthians 11:23-34.* The accounting records also are periodically examined to see if they are in balance. The test of the system's balance is called a trial balance. Until a proper trial balance is made, the accountant can be in error and not know it. So it is with our spiritual lives. Periodically, we need to stop and gain perspective, evaluate our lives, and determine if we are in balance with the will of God for our lives.

MERCHANDISING OPERATIONS 1: INVENTORY

WHAT DOES OUR SPIRITUAL INVENTORY LOOK LIKE? Jesus describes us as being fruit-bearing trees and branches. *Read Matthew 7:15-20.* If our heart, soul, strength, and mind are committed to God, we will produce good fruit. If we are rotten on the inside, we will produce bad fruit. Jesus said, "Thus, by their fruit you will recognize them" (NIV). What kind of fruit are you bearing for the Kingdom of God?

MERCHANDISING OPERATIONS 2

Read Luke 19:11-27. The concept of trading, buying low, and selling high is described in this passage, commonly known as the "Parable of the Talents." This passage might illustrate the investment of spiritual gifts. Most often in scripture, however, our spiritual inventory is not described as something we purchase and then sell. Instead, it is more like the inventory of the farmer, through which seeds grow into a harvest if they are properly planted and watered. *Read John 15:1-2 and 2 Corinthians 9:6-11.* Sometimes we plant, and sometimes we water. Our challenge is to sow generously in order to reap generously.

MERCHANDISING OPERATIONS 3

DOES GOD USE A PERIODIC OR PERPETUAL INVENTORY SYSTEM? In God's accounting system, humans became accounts receivable after the fall. The inventory of the earth is under His constant care. *Read Matthew 10:29-31.* Consider the number of people on the earth and the number of hairs on each head. Can God do exponential math or what? Jesus indicated that God uses a perpetual inventory system.

FULL DISCLOSURE

Financial reporting requires full disclosure. This means that significant events and financial transactions that could influence a decision-maker must be explained in the financial statement or its footnotes. But how are we to handle spiritual reporting to each other? *Read Matthew 6:1-6.* In God's system of spiritual reporting, He knows all and sees all. But in reporting to each other, the system is just the opposite of full disclosure. We are, in fact, to keep our good deeds a secret from friends and, if married, even from our spouses. The left hand should not know the good deeds of the right hand.

PRINCIPLES OF COST-BENEFIT, CONTROL, COMPATIBILITY, AND FLEXIBILITY

Accounting software supports operations and is essential to the continued growth of the company. Computer system design follows four principles: cost-benefit, control, compatibility, and flexibility. The same principles hold true for evaluating the church fellowship to which we belong. *Read Ephesians 5:10.* Questions about fellowship and where we belong in the Kingdom are some of the most difficult spiritual questions we face on this earth. Paul's admonition was to pray and search for God's will in our lives.

SUBSIDIARY LEDGERS

Accounting systems use subsidiary ledgers to group accounts receivable, accounts payable, inventory, and so on. Does God use subsidiary ledgers? *Read Revelation 20:11-12.* Yes, the book of life is a subsidiary ledger. Pray that your name is found in the book of life!

BANK RECONCILIATION

Bank reconciliations are a reality check. The bank statement generally is the transactional truth, and our accounting records are adjusted to conform to the economic reality of the bank. *Read 2 Corinthians 5:18-19.* Paul wrote, "God...gave us the ministry of reconciliation" (NIV). There is a spiritual reality that God will punish sin. There is also the reality that God has reconciled the world to Himself through Jesus Christ. The accountant has a duty to reconcile the company books to the economic reality of the bank's transactions. We, as Christians, have a ministry of reconciliation between the world and God the Father.

INTERNAL CONTROL

Internal control is absolutely critical for a business to function according to management's established procedures and policies. What are God's internal controls in your life that keep you true to Him? Internal control policies include but are not limited to the following:

AUTHORIZATION—The Bible "judges the thoughts and attitudes of the heart" (NIV). *Read Hebrews 4:12-13.*

RECORDING TRANSACTIONS—The Holy Spirit helps us determine what is sin. *Read Acts 5:3.*

DOCUMENTS AND RECORDS—An all-knowing God does not need to keep records. Yet in our own lives of producing fruit, we are not to record or show our good deeds.

LIMITED ACCESS—Our conscience helps us to limit our exposure to sin and to know what is good and beneficial for spiritual growth.

PERIODIC INDEPENDENT VERIFICATION—As brothers and sisters in Christ, we hold each other accountable for what is good and pure and holy.

SEPARATION OF DUTIES—Each of us in the Kingdom has a calling, a duty to perform. We are not all feet or hands.

SOUND PERSONNEL POLICIES—Choose your friends wisely, for "a companion of fools suffers harm" (Proverbs 13:20, NIV).

THE CREDIT DILEMMA

Every business is concerned about the time it takes to collect accountants receivable. We call this ratio "days sales outstanding," or DSO. The critical factor affecting this ratio is the companies' credit policies. Trusting everyone with unlimited credit will guarantee business failure. *Read Matthew 5:38-42 and Proverbs 22:26-27.* On the one hand, Jesus calls upon us to be very generous in our policies of lending. You are to love your enemies and lend to the person who wants to borrow from you. You also are encouraged from the passage in Proverbs not to provide the collateral or inventory for debt. Setting credit policy is a very difficult area for Christians who want to trust everyone while securing the financial health of their businesses.

SHORT-TERM INVESTMENTS

Short-term investments fall into one of three categories: trading securities, available-for-sale securities, or held-to-maturity Securities. <u>What type of security are you, spiritually speaking?</u> We all would like to be in the "held-to-maturity" category. Staying faithful to God takes reliance upon Him and emotional strength and commitment. *Read Romans 7:14-25.* We all want to strive mightily against sin. Yet often we fail in the struggle, and we realize our own weaknesses at that point. Unfortunately, the struggle does not get easier with age. For most people, emotional strength decreases with age. For example, as we age, we cry at events that never would have affected us in our youth. Only by the power of God can we remain faithful for a lifetime.

ALLOWANCE FOR DOUBTFUL ACCOUNTS

Every business is forced to face the fact that every customer is not going to pay his or her bill—some due to a lack of financial resources and others due to their swindling nature. To quote King David in Psalm 37:21, "The wicked borrow and do not repay" (NIV). Even believers, in dealing with each other, have a sinful nature. To quote Paul, "For all have sinned and fall short of the glory of God" (Romans 3:23, NIV). The correct accounting treatment is to create an allowance for doubtful accounts and estimate the amount of nonpayment. *Read 1 John 1:5-10.* The good news is that God will not fail us. He is trustworthy yesterday, today, and tomorrow. He is a consistent friend and source of power and light for doing good in our lives. We serve an awesome God!

INVENTORY 1

We are part of God's inventory. Can you name God's asset list from Genesis 1? heavens, earth, and light air ("sky") land, seas, and vegetation the sun, moon, and stars water creatures and birds land creatures and humans God rested!

Read Genesis 2:15. God gave to mankind a charge to work the earth and care for it. After the fall of mankind, the ground was cursed; then entered painful toil, thorns, and thistles into the human experience

(Genesis 3:17-18). Human beings confuse possession with ownership. God gave us possession of the earth, but it still belongs to Him. Humans are the caretakers, not the owners. In Leviticus 25:23 God said, "The land is mine and you are but aliens and my tenants" (NIV). This fact also speaks to the environmental debate. Regrettably, many people choose to ignore the environmental crisis, while others go to the opposite extreme and see created things as gods. "Mother Nature" has taken on a spirituality of her own, and defining her has become a religion.

INVENTORY 2

God created us as inventory; after the fall, we were reclassified as accounts receivable. Do we still belong to God? Do our bodies belong to Him? *Read 1 Corinthians 6:20.* What does it mean to honor God with your body? How you answer the question of ownership will determine your position on the abortion issue. If we own our bodies, then a mother has the right to terminate the life within her. If it is God's body, the mother's rights are limited to His rules and principles. Respect for life at conception is a sound biblical principle.

INVENTORY 3

Does God use a LIFO or FIFO inventory system? *Read Matthew 19:30; 20:1-16; Mark 10:31; or Luke 13:30*: "There are those who are last who will be first, and first who will be last" (NIV). God uses a LIFO system. What does this mean? We can infer from Matthew 20 that those who accept God early in the history of the Kingdom will be last in line, and those who accept God at the end of the period will be the first to enter heaven. Is this what these passages teach us?

LONG-TERM ASSETS 1

Jesus is not against investing in long-term assets. He is against investing in the wrong long-term assets. Repeatedly the scriptures encourage us to lay up treasure in heaven. *Read John 14:1-3.* Is the place Jesus is preparing for us a room in God's house or a mansion of our own? The translators of the King James Bible used the word "mansion" to represent the place prepared for the saints, and songs such as "Mansion just over the hilltop" made the idea popular.[4] <u>Do you expect to find great personal wealth in heaven?</u>

LONG-TERM ASSETS 2

Land tenure was everything in Old Testament times. Real wealth, or what was known as a true estate, was only real if it included land. Hence the term a "real estate." *Read Leviticus 25:23-28.* God was very concerned about property rights and the wealth it controlled. Is this how we define wealth today? No, today intangible assets compose most of our modern wealth. We use the expression "capitalization" to refer to modern wealth. "Equity capitalization" is the market price of the shares multiplied by the number of shares outstanding. Shares are intangible assets that define a legal right. The critical question is, "To what extent is this wealth the product of injustice?" We have a moral responsibility to analyze the profit-making activities and the social agendas of the corporations in which we invest.

LONG-TERM ASSETS 3

Often the ownership of assets is a disputed

[4] "Mansion Over the Hilltop" by Ira Stanphill, #881, Songs of Faith & Praise, Alton H. Howard, 1997.

accounting issue. Leases, for example, can be operating leases or capital leases. Capital leases are recorded on the balance sheet, and operating leases are not. Scripture teaches that our bodies are not our own; the earth and everything in it belongs to God. What about your soul? <u>Do you own your soul? Can you sell it to the devil?</u> *Read John 13:21-30.* What protection do you have against Satan? Two of the most difficult chapters in the Bible, Romans 9 and 10, address the relationship between God, humans, and Satan. Actually, we should read Romans 9, 10, and 11 together for a full understanding of free will and predestination. We have the indwelling and protection of the Holy Spirit for our souls. God holds the title, and we have unlimited use of this asset. Our souls are an operating lease from God.

DEFERRED GAINS AND LOSSES

One of the most complex topics in the revelation of God is deferred redemption. The Old Testament atonement process is described in Leviticus 4 and 16. *Read Romans 3:21-31.* The New Testament writers tell us that sins before the death of Jesus Christ were unpunished; they were deferred until the time of Christ. This is a difficult concept. So is the concept of deferred gains and losses for like-kind exchanges. Deferred gains and suspended losses are reflected in adjustments to basis. Like Old Testament sins, they are suspended in time, waiting for redemption to occur.

DEBT 1: GOD'S LIABILITY ACCOUNT

The scriptures consistently equate sin with debt. We owe God for our trespasses, what we call "sin." Jesus came to "forgive us our debts, as we also have forgiven our debtors" (Matthew 6:12, NIV). *Read Matthew 18:23-35.* It is very interesting to study cultural patterns of perception toward debt. In Jesus' time, debt could mean imprisonment. There are no debtors' prisons in the United States, but U.S. culture still debates the proper punishment for debt as defined in U.S. bankruptcy laws.

DEBT 2: IDEAL CAPITAL STRUCTURE

Is debt good or bad? Excessive credit card debt has become a financial epidemic in some cultures. Nonprofit organizations offering debt counseling abound. What is the proper attitude for a Christian to have toward debt? *Read Romans 13:1-10.* Paul encouraged us not to be in debt to anyone for anything, except to carry a debt of love for each other. To be totally debt-free should be a personal financial goal. In the world of corporate finance, the most profitable debt level depends on the stability of earnings over time; hence, the debt rating or cost of debt. For a company, an ideal capital structure balancing both debt and equity can contribute significantly to earnings. The ideal capital structure for an individual or family in U.S. culture often means the assumption of a mortgage and home ownership. Over time, home ownership also can contribute significantly to savings.

DEBT 3: REPAYMENT PERIOD

For how long a time period should we finance debt? The Old Testament law contained a redemption principle for debt every seven years, which included returning land to its original holders every fifty years. *Read Deuteronomy 15:1-6 and Leviticus 25:8-12.* Should we forgive debt every seven years? Jesus Christ fulfilled the Jubilee concept of debt forgiveness. Luke 4:18-19 records Jesus, at the beginning of His ministry, reading scripture in the synagogue in order to tell the audience that he was the personification of the year of Jubilee. Jesus came to earth as a man to free us from the chains of sin and death. As followers of Jesus Christ, we have the same mission. We become the reverse of mortgage brokers. We tell others how to be debt-free!

PARTNERSHIPS

Partnerships were a common business entity in New Testament times. John and James (the sons of Zebedee) and Simon Peter were in a partnership. *Read Luke 5:6-11.* Like Simon Peter, John, and James, we are called to join a partnership that fishes for lost souls. How do you feel about the term "partner" versus that of the term "brother or sister"? Paul used the term "partner" when referring to Christians with whom he had a working relationship—for example, Titus (2 Corinthians 8:23) and Philemon, the master of Onesimus (Philemon 17). Is this a good biblical term that we should use today?

CORPORATE FORM

What is the meaning of the term "incarnation"? The word means, "to take human form." When God became man, Jesus was the incarnation. How human was Jesus? Could he miss the nail with a hammer and smash this finger? Did he ever trip and fall down? *Read Mark 11:12-14.* The word "incorporate" means, "to make into a body." A corporation is a creature created by state statute. It is a type of incarnation. It is the assumption of a body by a legal entity that is then owned and directed by the shareholders. What we look forward to is the reverse of incarnation, when the church is transformed into the bride of Christ.

COMMON SHAREHOLDERS

We are shareholders in heaven. But are we common shareholders or preferred shareholders? Consider our rights as shareholders. We have no votes, and we are callable souls in God's eyes. This means we hold convertible preferred shares and are looking forward to being called and converted. Dividends can be considered gifts by the shareholders. Does God pay dividends? Peter said that we receive the gift of the Holy Spirit when we accept the Lord in baptism (Acts 2:38). The difference between corporate dividends and spiritual dividends is that the spiritual dividends are not proportionate to the number of shares we hold. *Read Ephesians 4:7-8.* Common translations for the way spiritual gifts are distributed are "apportioned" and "allocated."

DISCONTINUED OPERATIONS

The income statement is divided into income from continuing operations and all other one-time events that happened during a particular year. Many companies also have discontinued operations, which usually are unprofitable activities that management wants to terminate. *Read Ephesians 4:22-24 and 1 Peter 1:14-16.* As Christians we are called "to put off your old self, which is being corrupted by its deceitful desires, to be made new in the attitude of your minds" (NIV). We are to discontinue the spiritually unproductive activities in our lives.

STATEMENT OF SHAREHOLDERS EQUITY

Business organizations generally fall into three organizational forms: sole proprietorship, partnership, or corporation. What kind of business form do you have as a Christian? Are you a sole proprietorship who tries to stand on your own? Are you a partner with God? In partnerships, the parties share an equality, and we know we cannot assume equality with God. In stead, God is the principal investor and uses the Holy Spirit and other people to mold and shape us into His image. *Read Isaiah 64:8-9 or 45:9.* In accounting, the "Statement of Shareholders' Equity" discloses the different types of investors in a corporation? What would your "Statement of Shareholders' Spiritual Equity" look like? What are the supporting ligaments of your spiritual growth? You might have one column for parents, one for teachers, and another for brothers and sisters in Christ. For all of us, the statement would include this disclaimer: "God is still working on me."

SHARE VALUE

The word "value" is perhaps the most overused term in finance. We hear questions such as "Does it add value?" or "Is the stock overvalued?" The term "Christian values" might be the most overused term on family radio.

During a time when values are in question, it is good to remind ourselves of the value God places on each one of us. *Read Matthew 10:31 or Luke 12:7.* Perhaps God's response to Jesus' baptism as recorded in Matthew 3:17 is the clearest answer we have to questions about our identity. God answered three questions for Jesus (NIV):

Who am I? "This is my Son."

What is our relationship? "Whom I love."

How am I doing? "With him I am well pleased."

Each believer needs to hear those same words from the Holy Spirit that dwells within him or her.

STATEMENT OF CASH FLOWS 1

A common expression in the corporate financial world is "Cash is King." Everyone knows that "cash concerns" rule. Employees will tolerate a lot of internal problems as long as their paychecks do not bounce. In the nonprofit sector, cash flow is even more important. *Read John 18:33-37.* The spiritual world has a King whose name is Jesus Christ. As Christians we are members of the Lord's Kingdom. <u>What difference has his kingship made in your life?</u>

STATEMENT OF CASH FLOWS 2

What would a standard distribution curve look like if all of Jesus' believers were placed on it according to their prayer life? The majority of Christians, centered around the mean, maintain a consistent prayer life. They find time to seriously study scripture, and they feed themselves with regular worship. They do not need continual spiritual investment by others. The left tail of the distribution curve most likely would be pastors who are so efficient in their spiritual operations that they can invest in the spiritual maintenance and support of others. The right side of the curve most likely would be those individuals who need continual emotional and spiritual support to remain faithful to God. They have negative spiritual operations that need to be financed by others. *Read Ephesians 4:14-17.* The business world divides the activities of an entity into three categories: operations, investments, and financing. Some businesses support themselves from operations. Others, like pastors, are efficient at operations and can make investments in fixed assets. Still others, like most of the "dot-com" companies, have negative operations and need continual financing by outsiders in order to survive.

Are your daily spiritual operations self-sufficient? Do you get enough time alone with God and in the fellowship of the saints to empower yourself spiritually?

STATEMENT OF CASH FLOWS 3

A positive cash flow from operations (CF Op.) is a measure of financial strength. Financial ratios, which use net income, also can be modified to assess the strength of cash flows by substituting CF Op. in place of net income. For example, the measure for margin is net income over sales. The ratio of CF Op. over sales produces a ratio similar to margin. What is a good measure of our spiritual strength? *Read Matthew 17:20-21.* Most Christians acknowledge that faith is the key to being strong for God. Imagine for a moment a tree in the morning sunshine after an ice storm the night before with all the branches covered in ice. The tree is blocking your view of the sun, but the branches covered in ice are refracting the sun's light. So it is with faith. Like the refractions of the sun's light, we only can see the evidence of faith. "Now faith is being sure of what we hope for and certain of what we do not see" (Hebrews 11:1). Pray that God gives you the faith to be strong!

FINANCIAL STATEMENT ANALYSIS 1

Anyone who has ever purchased a used car knows that the perception often is not the final reality. There are generally significant problems with a used car that are not perceived before the purchase is made. The same can be said for purchasing "used" shares. Shares purchased on an organized exchange are previously owned and are, therefore, used. With used cars and shares of stock, the front-end perception often is better than the final result or end perception. Minimizing the difference between perception and reality is the purpose of financial statement analysis. The attempt is to remove surprises by thoroughly studying the company's strategic analysis and available financial data. Likewise, we should carefully analyze new activities in our lives. Like the used car or that "perfect" stock pick, sin looks better on the front-end than on the back-end. The old adage "The grass looks greener on the other side" holds true when we choose what looks like the easy path over God's will for our lives. *Read Luke 15:11-32*, commonly knows as the "Parable of the Lost Son." The father in the story represents God the Father, and the good news is that He welcomes us back home after a reckless lifestyle. Sin always looks better on the front-end than on the back-end.

FINANCIAL STATEMENT ANALYSIS 2

There are five primary factors we use to evaluate shares of corporate stock: risk, technical analysis, value, liquidity, and profitability. (And there are six factors if you include prayer.) What factors do we use to evaluate the investment of our time in godly activities? *Read 2 Timothy 3:14-17*. Most faith groups use the Bible to rule out certain activities, and other groups use the Bible to rule in activities. All Christian faith groups, including the Roman Catholic Church, search the scriptures for commands, examples, and necessary inferences. Are we commanded in the scriptures to build houses for the poor, as do volunteers for Habitat for Humanity? No! However, it certainly is a necessary inference to "love your neighbor as yourself." Evaluating the use of our time and our money requires considerable wisdom from above.

Praying before a share purchase or a commitment of volunteer time will help to create value.

SHARE PRICE

The formula for share price is Price = $D_1/(k-g)$. Why does the formula use D_1, the future dividend, instead of D_0, the current dividend? Because the share-price formula is a derivative of the present value formula, $PV = FV/(1+k)n$. The stock market bases the share price on the future performance of the company, not on the present performance. So it is with the Christian life. Our definition of value is based upon a belief in future events, not present events. Elton Trueblood wrote a book titled *A Place to Stand*.[5] The resurrection of Jesus Christ is our place to stand. *Read John 11:25-26.* Where is your place to stand?

Change in Accounting Principles

Sometimes a business must acknowledge that an accounting practice they have been using is not in the best interest of fair disclosure. AOL, for example, booked its distribution of free trial disks as an asset instead of as an expense. Through pressure from the financial community, AOL took a one-time hit and corrected the financial statements. Share price increased as a result. *Read 1 John 1:8-10.* Salvation is all about coming clean. Acknowledging and confessing our sins is the beginning point for the cleansing that comes from the blood of Jesus Christ.

INTERNATIONAL ACCOUNTING STANDARDS

What do we mean by the expression "The world is

---

[5] Trueblood, Eton, A Place to Stand, Harper & Row Publishers, N.Y., 1969.

getting smaller?" What kinds of businesses are forced to think and act globally? Consider the percentage of foreign revenues for some major U.S. companies: Exxon, 77%; General Motors, 31%; Mobil, 67%; IBM, 61%.[6]

Did Jesus have a global perspective? Yes! He instructed his disciples to take his message to the whole world (Matthew 28:19-20). Perhaps the clearest example of Jesus' global perspective is the so-called "Parable of the Good Samaritan," in which the hero is a foreigner. *Read Luke 10:25-37.* The "love-your-neighbor" principle is universal. We have a moral obligation to care about people we have never met who suffer from poverty and affliction. Lord, give us your eyes for the poor.

BUSINESS CONSOLIDATIONS AND MINORITY INTEREST

Business consolidations should be an attempt to add value to each company. Occasionally they do succeed in raising the share prices of both companies. The resulting combination is a larger and hopefully more economically successful operation. The parent corporation can purchase the shares in a friendly "takeover" arranged between the two boards of directors or in a hostile manner often resulting in a bidding war between rivals. The shares not obtained by the parent are called the "minority interest." There are several parallels in the spiritual realm. *Read 1 Corinthians 6:19-20.* Jesus paid for our sins on the cross, and we become one with Him in a consolidated relationship. For some believers, it is a friendly merger nurtured by parents and Bible schoolteachers. For others, it seems to be an all-out fight between the forces of God and the forces of Satan. Successful

[6] Forbes, July 28, 1997, "The 100 Largest U. S. Multinationals."

contributions from God, parents, and children (the subsidiary entity) always increase value. Our consolidated statements then reflect God's ownership control in our lives, and the minority interest indicates the portions of our lives that we hold back, unwilling to give to God.

EQUITY METHOD

The equity method is unique to the financial landscape of the United States. It follows the notion that "we are they, and they are us." When the investment target has earnings, the investor has earnings. When the investment target pays dividends, the value of the investor's investment decreases. Consider the relationship between brothers and sisters in Christ. We follow a similar equity principle. *Read 1 Corinthians 12:12-20.* We cry with those who grieve and rejoice with those who are joyful. We treat each other as family. We are they, and they are us; we are one body. We influence each other, but we do not control each other; this is the equity method of spirituality.

GOODWILL OR GOD'S WILL

Providence is a biblical concept, and so is predestination. *Read Romans 8:28-30.* God has a plan for each of us, and we pray for a spirit of revelation to know and understand His will for our lives. Most Christians say that it is by His grace (providence) that they enjoy the abundant blessings of life. These abundant blessings are "extras" that come as a result of being purchased by the blood of Jesus Christ. In accounting language, excess value that arises from a purchase is termed "goodwill." The difference is in who paid the price.

INTRODUCTION TO MANAGEMENT ACCOUNTING

Is work good? Is it good to get up each morning and go to work? Does it benefit us spiritually, mentally, and physically to actively earn a living? The people of Haiti are descendants of Africans forced into slave labor, and they have a saying about work: "If work was good, the white man would have done it." The Bible tells us that work is good because it is a godly activity. *Read Genesis 2:1-3.* Humans were created as creatures of work (Genesis 2:15), as God told man to "work [the Garden of Eden] and take care of it" (NIV). Work gives purpose and meaning to our lives. It is interesting that people of different ages answer the question "Is work good?" differently. Twenty-year-old college students almost always will say "yes," but older students taking evening classes often question the principle as they start looking forward to retirement. What is wrong with playing golf five times a week?

WORK WITH YOUR HANDS

What is the significance of working with your hands? Is working with physical things superior to working mentally in God's eyes? Is physical work of a higher calling or more satisfying? Different cultures will answer these questions differently. In some of the former Soviet nations, only physical work was considered to provide an honest living. Buying low and selling high (merchandising) was not an honorable way to make a living. Even in the United States, trading shares of stock was considered a dishonorable profession until after the Great Depression and the creation of the SEC.[7] *Read 1 Thessalonians 4:11-12.* We are commanded to "work with your hands." Does it

[7] "Easy but Sleazy," Bridget O'Brian, Wall Street Journal, Tuesday, May 28, 1996.

make a difference to God if we work with our hands or with our minds?

TRANSFORMED LIVES, OUR SPIRITUAL PRODUCT

Consider for a moment the spiritual product we produce—transformed lives. In accounting, material, labor, and overhead go into each product. Spiritually, we can think of the Word of God that became flesh as the material and the work of the Holy Spirit as the labor. *Read John 6:35-45.* As God teaches, He draws us to him in the conversion process. <u>What is our role in the conversion process? Are we also direct labor, or are we indirect labor and part of overhead? Are Christian colleges and church buildings overhead?</u> I would suggest that Christians be considered indirect labor. We are overhead in the process of transforming lives. Evangelism is not salesmanship. Conversion is not our closing the sale. We carry and deliver the message, but God works within each heart to bring about change.

THE GOAL OF MANAGEMENT ACCOUNTING: WEALTH CREATION THROUGH PRODUCTION

The problem with successful operations is that they can separate us from God; the temptation is to believe that our success is a result of our own power and intellect. *Read Deuteronomy 8:17-20:* "For it is he who gives you the ability to produce wealth" (NIV). Do we live by our own strength and trust in our bank accountants, or do we trust in God? Second Samuel 24 recounts how King David counted the fighting men. God considered this a great trespass because it did not reflect complete trust and dependence upon Him. In this context, accounting once was considered an evil activity.

IS MANUFACTURING A GODLY ACTIVITY?

Are we created by a builder to be builders? *Read Genesis 1:31:* "God saw all that he had made, and it was very good" (NIV). God is the ultimate builder. We were created in His image, so we also are created to be builders. From children to adults, people love to construct, weave, and assemble. For some, this is reflected in activities such as gardening or preparing food. For others, this is reflected in physical construction or in the entrepreneurial activity of building a business. Whatever the medium, we love to build.

THE USE OF STANDARDS

Managerial accounting uses non-financial standards to measure performance. Management and employees (or their unions) often debate these standards. So it is in the spiritual realm. Standards are hotly debated. The timing and meaning of baptism, for example, is one of the most debated standards. Many people say baptism in water is required for salvation (Acts 2:38-41), while others say only grace saves us (Galatians 3:1-9). By what standards does God judge us? *Read Matthew 5:21-22.* Jesus outlines perfection in the so-called "Sermon on the Mount," recorded in Matthew 5–7. What source do you use to determine godly standards?

ACTIVITY-BASED COSTING

The accounting method that assigns cost to a specific activity is called activity-based costing, or ABC. The activities are grouped into cost pools, and each cost pool has a cost driver. Total overhead for the product is determined by the use of each cost pool. The goal of ABC is to eliminate non-value-added activities.

The spiritual life includes many activities that contribute to spiritual growth and many that are not value-added, which reduce our spirituality. Like the accounting technique of ABC, we must continually evaluate our activities and determine their costs. *Read Matthew 16:24-28:* "What good will it be for a man if he gains the whole world, yet forfeits his soul?" (NIV). We can be consumed with activities—even good activities that help others—that sacrifice our own time with God. The wise person will discern the difference between life's value-added activities and non-value-added activities.

QUESTIONABLE PRODUCTS

Can a faithful Christian produce wine? The answer is "yes" because the Lord Jesus Christ Himself created wine. *Read John 2:1-11.* The Gospel is compared to new wine, and Paul encouraged Timothy to use a little wine for his stomach's sake. But drunkenness is a sin, and the number of lives that have been ruined by excessive consumption is horrific. With alcoholic beverages, people either like the feeling (the "buzz") or they don't. If you like the feeling of losing control, drinking is a problem for you. The production of questionable products falls under the admonition of the Apostle Paul in 1 Corinthians 10:23: " 'Everything is permissible'—but not everything is beneficial" (NIV).

PROCESS COSTING OR JOB-ORDER COSTING OR BOTH?

Does God use a job-order costing system or a process costing system? If sin has a spiritual cost per person, God uses a job-order system. *Read Mark 2:8-12.* We each are accountable for our own sins. What about the sins of a nation? Does God accumulate the sins of a nation and then hold all of the citizens accountable, as in process costing? Do you worry about and pray for forgiveness for the sins of your nation?

SHARE DIVIDENDS.

Most shareholders are pleased to receive a share dividend because they think it has multiplied their ownership of the company. The truth is that they received nothing of value. Their percentage ownership of the company is still the same after the dividend as it was before the dividend. Dividends are gifts from corporations. Cash poor corporations give share dividends to keep shareholders happy. God gives us dividends or truly wonderful gifts as shareholders in the kingdom of God. One of the promises to the Children of Israel was the multiplying of their days on this earth if they fixed their eyes, hearts and minds on the word of God (Deut 11:21ff). Christians don't have the same promise of a longer earthly life, but we do have the promise of salvation and home with Jesus in heaven.

SHARE SPLITS.

Share splits are necessary to keep the price per share under $100. The financial markets are not required to do so but it does facilitate trading. Trades between investment bankers and the financial markets like the NYSE are always done in round lots of 100 shares. A price per share of over $100 means the total amount traded on round lots is over $10,000. Splits are a means of dividing the price into a more manageable amount. Do we have splits in our ownership of heavenly shares? Jesus said to divide the cup and bread when he gave instructions about the Lord's Communion (Luke 22:17). Dividing our communion bread and all other forms of wealth and ownership is required for good Christian stewardship. Sharing the gospel message is a form of share splitting. Yet the more we give away spiritually the more we have. God's economy is very different from financial markets.

SIN IS BOTH A FIXED COST AND A VARIABLE COST

The price of any product can be divided into both fixed costs and variable costs. The fixed costs include overhead items such as rent and depreciation, all of the costs that create the environment in which the product will be constructed. The variable costs include labor, materials and variable overhead. Sin also has a variable component and a fixed component. Consider I Corinthians 15:22 *"For as in Adam all die, so in Christ all will be made alive."* We are born into the sinful condition of humanity or what theologians call original sin. This is our fixed cost, the environment into which we are born. Then we add sins of our own or variable costs. The Old Testament teaches that the sins of the father were passed on for four generations (Exodus 20:5, 34:7). This is why Jesus had to be born of a virgin. Mothers do not pass on their sins, only fathers. If Jesus had an earthly father He would have had original sins from that father. The promise to Christians is that we are not responsible for the sins of our fathers, only the sin of Adam (Jeremiah 31:30).

BUDGETING

To budget is just good business. Count the costs ahead of time to decide if the project is financially feasible. Does Jesus believe in budgeting? Luke 14:28 *"Suppose one of you wants to build a tower. Will he not first sit down and estimate the cost to see if he has enough money to complete it."* Following Jesus has a cost. Are you willing to pay the price? Does Jesus want

10% of our net or gross income? What is the budgeted cost? Jesus said: *"any of you who does not give up everything he has cannot be my disciple"* Luke 14:33. Jesus wants 100% of our possessions and 100% of our hearts to follow Him.

FLEXIBLE BUDGETS

Most organizations make their budget plans based on all available information at a point in time. If the budget is adjusted for changes in the volume of production, it is called a flexible budget, if not, it is a static budget. For example, a university will make a budget many months in advance of the fall enrollment. What if the enrollment is larger than expected such that more classes need to be offered? Does the department level budgets change to reflect the increase (a flexible budget) or are the same number of classes offered (static budget) forcing students to take classes they are not interested in taking. Obviously, the flexible budget is preferable to anyone who faces production issues. Does God use a static budget or a flexible budget? In other words, are different groups of people evaluated differently depending on their training, experiences or calling in life? James 3:1 **"Not many of you should presume to be teachers, my brothers, because you know that we who teach will be judged more strictly."** It would appear that God uses a flexible budget to judge our faults.

INCOME TAXES, A PAY-AS-YOU-GO SYSTEM

The IRS is very insistent on a pay-as-you-go system to collect taxes. This is why payroll taxes are withheld before the paycheck is disbursed. Independent contractors and investors must also make regular payments to the IRS on a quarterly basis. The due dates are April 15th, June 15th, September 15th and January 15th of the following year. The logic is very simple. If one large payment was permitted on April 15th instead of regular payments, the taxpayer might not have sufficient funds in reserve to make the payment. The Apostle Paul used the same logic. He asked the Corinthian church to collect God's money on a pay-as-you-go system. *"On the first day of every week, each one of you should set aside a sum of money in keeping with his income, saving it up, so that when I come no collections will have to be made"* I Corinthians 16:2. Notice that the amount of the contribution was proportional to income instead of a flat 10%. The idea of a 10% contribution is an Old Testament concept not duplicated in God's New Covenant with His people.

Chapter 14

A THEOLOGY OF SUFFERING

YOU CAN BUILD A CAPACITY FOR SUFFERING

By Dr. Jack E. Bower

Why should I devote a chapter on theology in a book on accounting? I consider it an editorial privilege. I want to give you - the student - an opportunity to consider some new ideas about suffering and, perhaps, improve upon your own theology of suffering. This chapter will spark some interesting class discussions if used as a reading assignment. C. S. Lewis is quoted as saying: *"God whispers to us in our pleasures, speaks to us in our conscience, but shouts in our pains: It is His megaphone to rouse a deaf world."*[1] My goal is to provide you additional journal entries in the general ledger of life. Just as you can master the skills for

---

[1] C.S. Lewis, *The Problem of Pain*, Harber, San Francisco, 2001, ISBN 0060652969

accounting or finance, you can also build a capacity for suffering, and thus suffer well when it happens to you. For those of you who do not know me as a professor, I have cancer. At the time of this writing I am in stable condition, for which I give to God all the glory. I am convinced that I am still able to write to you only because of those brothers and sisters in Christ who are praying for me. Let me explain why I believe so strongly in prayer. I received several series of different types of chemotherapy treatments. The many rounds of chemotherapy unfortunately did not affect my cancer and my condition deteriorated rapidly. My church held a day of fasting and prayer for me on the last day that I was able to receive a chemotherapy treatment. That last treatment was the turning point for me. My health improved as the cancer sites began to shrink. I am not yet in remission, but God has been merciful to me. (See Philippians 2:27.)

The theology of suffering is a popular topic. I act as if Google is my second brain, since I use it for seemingly everything in accounting and finance, even for those sites that have their own search engine like irs.gov. A Google search will yield over 300,000 hits on the topic of the theology of suffering. It is so prevalent because every one who is alive will experience suffering of some type before they die. One of my favorite books on this topic is *How the Soul Goes Though Loss,* by Gerald Sitter. Another is *The Problem of Pain*, by C. S. Lewis. Both Calvin and Luther addressed suffering. Calvin thought it a useful agent of God. I am certainly not such a proponent, although I do appreciate their perspective. I believe that God allows suffering in our lives to help mold and shape us into the image of Jesus Christ.

An explanation of suffering is in order before I

continue. Suffering is the death of a loved one; the loss of an unborn child or offspring; a difficult marriage or divorce; unbearable pain, illness, or an untreatable disease. The list is endless. In one sense, we are all terminally ill. Being healthy is just the slowest way to meet the Lord.

The spiritual battle rages and leads to the question, "Why me?" Chemotherapy treatments are received in a room full of people in various stages of cancer. Each individual is attached to injection pumps that dispense toxic chemicals intravenously at a metered rate. The chemotherapy then proceeds to indiscriminately kill all cells in the body. The theory is that if you survive the chemotherapy treatments, normal cells will re- grow (mitosis) and cancer cells, once destroyed, will not. My cancer was diagnosed at stage four, the final stage of lymphoma when it was widespread and had metastized in my Bone marrow. The infusions lasted over eight hours, so the "Chemo Room" became a sanctuary of friends, a place to get to know fellow victims of this dreaded disease. Everyone I spoke with told me the same thing: The spiritual battle of "Why me?" was much more difficult to endure than the suffering inflicted by the cancer or the chemotherapy treatments. The mystery of "Why me?" is as old as the history of mankind. Many scholars believe that Job is the oldest book of the Hebrew Bible. The story of Job is his spiritual battle of "Why me?" What was true for the other patient was not true for me: I was never alone. I attribute that to the unknown number of people who prayed and continue to pray for me. A strange sense of the presence of God comes over you – an awareness that you are never alone - when people pray for you.

Is it wrong to ask "Why me?" Certainly not! We all want to know why bad things happen to good people. Jesus gave an excellent condensed version of the story of Job with the account of the people killed by the Tower in Siloam. (Luke 13). He asked those around Him, "Do you think they (*that is, those killed by the Tower of Siloam* (emphasis mine)) were more guilty than all the others living in Jerusalem?" The answer from the Son of God was an unambiguous, "No!" Jesus addressed the fundamental question of the connection between suffering and sin. Jesus says that those who suffer are not the greatest sinners. This was the problem with the friends of Job: They wanted to blame his suffering on some un-confessed sin in his life. It does make sense at first glance. The old expression, "They got what they deserved", contains a certain element of truth. However, if this were a universal spiritual principle, then the wicked would be poor and sick while the righteous would be wealthy and possess good health. We need only to look at the final years of the twelve apostles to understand that the people of God do indeed suffer as a part of their spiritual transformation.

REVERSE ADULTHOOD?

Being terminally ill has taught me to read the scriptures with a unique perspective. As an example, for most of my life I did not fully understand the implication of Matt 18:3. "*I tell you the truth, unless you change and become like little children you will never enter the kingdom of God.*" "Never" seems like a very convincing word. After all, I work in an intellectual community that has as learning objectives both spiritual formation and spiritual maturity. Eastern University attempts to transform students into more mature individuals infused with a greater appreciation of the world around them. Becoming childlike would seem to be going the wrong direction. Does Jesus want us to exchange adulthood for some other state of mind?

A NEW DEFINITION OF FAITH:

Let me now postulate as to what I think Jesus was saying in Luke 13. Cancer has given me a new perspective on faith. By faith, I now accept as truth, that God knows more about life than I do. God sent a grandchild named Joshua into my life and, along with him, time for reflection to learn the substance of real faith. What God wants from us is a childlike trust. Joshua is not always happy with the parameters his parents have for play and sleep. One might be led to ask just how much control does Joshua actually have over this world? He thinks he is the center of the universe. My wife Wendy jokingly says that it is a shame he has not yet learned to snap his fingers. Is Joshua in control just because he thinks he is? Of course not! Can we control God? Of course not! And that is the moral lesson in the story of Job. Like my grandson, Joshua, we may think that we are in control, but that approach is just an illusion based on an incomplete understanding of reality. Our perceptions of reality must appear childlike to God.

Note the symbolism in the scripture story of the sheep and the shepherd. I doubt that they understand the need for the shepherd to bathe them in order to remove vermin from their wool. Wendy and I provide food for several feral cats and other wildlife. I often comment to her that the cats are the dumbest in the world. But then I stop and think that God probably says the same thing about me. That is, Jack Bower must be the dumbest human being he ever created. He (Jack) just does not understand how I involve myself in his life. The comparison of my intelligence to that of feral cats fails to approximate the distance between myself and God vis-à-vis our intellect. This is also the conclusion to the story of Job. God says to Job, "Where were you when I laid the earth's foundation? Tell me if you understand? Who marked off the dimensions, surely you know?" The failure of Job to understand his suffering was based on his own intellectual limitations. Read Job chapters 38 to 42 for additional insight regarding the attitude of humility.

In chapter 55, verse 8, of the book he wrote, the prophet Isaiah also said it well, "Who are we to comprehend the vastness of God." Look at the life of Jesus Christ. In my human wisdom, his time on earth was far too brief. I would have had him preach several sermons on the mount and extend His earthly ministry for twenty or more years! We just do not know the timing of God.

A CULTURAL SHIFT IN THE U.S:

The seal of Harvard University provides valuable insight into a cultural shift that has taken place in the United States as it pertains to the mind of God. The seal contains a crest with three books. The first is labeled VE, the second, RI, and the third, at the bottom of the crest, is labeled TAS. In 1650, the seal read "For the Glory of Christ." That changed in 1692 to "Truth for Christ and the Church." The early seals also displayed the bottom book labeled TAS as being face down. This book contained the secret things of God unavailable to mankind. Today the inscriptions referring to "Christ" and "His Church" have been removed. Even more interesting is that the third book is now facing up. Our society believes it has the right to know everything. We attempt to reveal the unknown with our scientific methods. One of the most difficult aspects of complete surrender to the will of God is that we will never know the "Why" until we get to heaven.

LIFE ON EARTH OR A JOB IN HEAVEN?

A best friend of mine died of cancer in his mid-thirties. His name was Robert Schubmehl. I still do not know why God called Bob home to heaven at such a young age. He had a fantastic youth ministry and was a leader in the church I attended. I certainly do not possess knowledge about the inner workings of heaven, but speculation is permissible. We serve a God who works. In fact, He never stops working. Jesus said that He works seven days a week. (John 5:16-18) It would be very strange if we could pray only six days a week because God rested on the Sabbath. God loves to create and He gave that gift to humans. We have a passion to build/create with our hands/minds as a result of being created in the image of God. Is heaven a place of rest? I believe so, but rest from what? I envision heaven as a haven of rest in our never-ending fight against evil. The writer of Hebrews encourages those believers to remain steadfast so that they can enter the rest of God.[2] Will we still be able to create in heaven? Will there be satisfying work for us to do? I would answer "Yes" to each of these questions. I picture God patiently waiting for us to arrive in heaven in order to start on the tasks He has prepared for us. I pray that mine will be playing a harp with the angel band. Perhaps God had a mission in mind for Bob Schubmehl that just

[2] Daniel, Fletcher. *Wandering and Resting: The Paradox of Sabbath Eschatology in Hebrews*, West Minster Seminary, 2004.

could not wait. Consider the possibility that your heavenly job is the real reason you were born in the first place. Read Matthews 25: 24ff: if you would like a proof text for job assignments in heaven. Note that verse 30 implies hell. That being so, verse 23 must imply heaven, *"Well done, good and faithful servant! You have been faithful with a few things;* **I will put you in charge of many things.** *Come and share your master's happiness!*

SUFFERING IS NECESSARY FOR SPIRITUAL TRANSFORMATION:

I grew up on a flood plain. My son, Jonathan, currently lives on a flood plain where the inconvenience of high water and the mud that follows is accepted as a way of life. People who live under these conditions do not say, "IF it floods"; rather, they declare "WHEN it floods." Consequently, it is not IF you will suffer, it is WHEN you will suffer. The only question now is "Will accept your suffering?"

I have come to the conclusion that suffering is a part of our spiritual transformation. We are called to be transformed into the image of Jesus Christ. I am convinced that God allows us to suffer to expose weaknesses in our character. Students, aware that I am dying from cancer, often come to my office at Eastern University to talk to me about death and dying, most often because they have just lost a loved one. An experience with death has motivated them to question their relationship with God. Their prayers did not persuade God to spare the life of their parent or best friend.

I had a similar experience when my best friend Bob Schubmehl died. I wondered why God did not answer my prayers. Many Christians and non-Christians prayed for Bob. I was certain until the day he died that he would be healed. At that time I did not understand the concept of total surrender to the will of God. That experience and my current circumstances have transformed both my faith in and relationship to God. I am convinced that suffering is necessary to affect the plan of transformation God has for my soul and the souls of countless others.

Great preparation is the key to survival for someone living on a river in a flood plain. The more prepared you are for a flood, the greater the likelihood that you will not experience either substantial loss or the need for significant cleanup.

The following is a good example of the benefit to preparation. My son and I recently installed an oil-fired furnace on the second floor of his house, eleven feet above ground level. Waters in that flood plain have never exceeded eleven feet to my knowledge. We placed the oil tank itself, however, on the first floor of his house. Most oil tanks rest on the floor about one-half full each of oil and air. That is enough air to float a tank that is half full of oil. Floating and leaking oil tanks present a significant environmental issue during a flood. We placed the legs of our oil tank in three yards of concrete, using two-inch wide bull chains to secure it to eye beams under the fireplace. Is there any possibility that the oil tank will break free during a flood? Probably not, but it illustrates the kind of preparation necessary when living on a flood plain.

I believe that preparation is fundamental for suffering well and that each one of us should strive to build our capacity to suffer. You will be ready when hard times come upon you if the groundwork of preparation is laid sooner rather than later. You can train yourself to think differently such that small habits become a life style.

I now understand that neither courage nor intellect is essential to survive suffering. What we need is to properly construct a house of faith that can stand firm when the floods of life assail us. "Therefore, everyone who hears these words of mine and puts them into practice is like a wise man who built his house on the rock. The rains came down, the streams rose, and the winds blew and beat against that house; yet it did not fall, because it had its foundation on the rock." Matt 7:24. Jesus taught that developing the right way of thinking about life is similar to the construction of a house. What we need is a strong foundation found only in the words and teaching of Jesus Christ.

I Samuel 17 tells the story of David and Goliath. In the account, David goes into battle against the giant with only a sling. But David needs ammunition, and so he selects five smooth stones from a brook. With these rudimentary weapons he goes forth and prevails over Goliath. God used those five stones for His glory. River stones are made smooth from continuous movement along the riverbed. Likewise, in our suffering we are buffeted by the trials and tribulations that come into our lives. Life not only wears us down but it can also make us submissive to and useful for the good purposes of God. And like David, all we need to do is believe in the transforming power of God.

Believing in God and in His power is akin to having flood insurance, only much better. Let me develop this analogy using the following order of events. First come the floodwaters, then the cleanup, and, next, contact with an insurance adjuster. We go through a process of gathering supporting documentation after which we file a damage report and insurance claim. A check was received from the insurance company in due time; our first was for approximately $20,000. It is cycle often repeated by those living in a flood plain: A house is damaged or destroyed by a flood only to be rebuilt better able to withstand the next torrent. Suffering certainly can destroy us. But like flood insurance, our God is always there to restore us through the Holy Spirit.

I have acquired a new way of looking at life as a result of my suffering. I now look at every experience as an opportunity for God to intervene in my life. A cancer patient regularly consults with a number of medical professionals. I sometimes visit in the same week with two or more MDs. When an appointment is cancelled, I simply respond that, perhaps, God did not want me to meet with that particular doctor. The office staff is usually surprised by my attitude. When I am delayed in traffic, I think to myself that, perhaps, God does not want me to get to a particular destination on time. Whatever the reason, I do not know and do not need to know. Life is full of so many more possibilities if you would leave yourself open to the providence of God.

I have sat at the proverbial feet of a number of great teachers during my lifetime and God continues to send them my way. I have appreciation for the sacrifice that many of them made to impact my life in a positive manner now that I am a teacher by profession. Suffering is one teacher that we neither love nor respect, though she does draw us closer to God. I often reflect on an Old Testament passage from the book of Isaiah, chapter 30, verse 20: *"Although the Lord gives you the bread of adversity and the water of affliction, your teachers will be hidden no more; with your own eyes you will see them. Whether you turn to the right or to the left, your ears will hear a voice behind you saying, "This is the way; walk in it."* Isaiah understood a basic principle he had learned in the "school of life," that God uses adversity and affliction to reveal His will for our lives. Graduate classes in the economic development program at Eastern University often include a significant percentage of international students. They are by and large puzzled by the attitude our culture has on suffering. A number of societies around the world believe that suffering is not only to be expected, but is accepted as a lesson from God. In fact, in some cultures there is an aura of nobility in suffering. How did we Americans develop such a different perspective from the rest of the world on this issue? One could begin with the U.S. Constitution which promises "life, liberty, and the pursuit of **happiness.**"

BUILDING PRODUCTIVE CAPACITY:
Stephen R. Covey wrote a now-famous book titled *The 7 Habits of Highly Effective People.* The theme of his book was identifying the distinction between production and the building of productive capacity. Simply stated, highly effective people build productive capacity. Covey retells the story of the goose that lays golden eggs. He notes that the egg is production and the goose is the productive capacity. His point is that one should never forget to feed the goose. The word of God is our food and production is our ability to deal with the problems of life. But we neglect to feed ourselves on the word of God and therefore loose productive capacity. Yet I am convinced that one can build a capacity to suffer well. Organized Living is a store for building personal productive capacity. The place for building spiritual productive capacity is called Bible Class.

JESUS AS OUR EXAMPLE:
Most Christians would claim that their goal is to

become more like Christ. Teenagers are taught to ask questions such as "What would Jesus do?" in a particular situation. Do you really want to be more like Jesus Christ? Then one must plan to suffer if the answer is in the affirmative. In some way it is love that calls us to suffering. You will feel the pain of others if your heart is tender and you show genuine care for them. Standing up against injustice or evil can be painful both mentally and physically. Whistle blowers usually suffer more than the wrongdoers. Take a look at the life of Jesus: A questionable birth; homelessness (i.e., no place to lay his head); betrayed by a friend; beaten and crucified unto death. *"To this you were called, because Christ **suffered for you**, leaving you an example, that you should follow in His steps."* I Peter 2:21.

The movie *The Passion of the Christ* was not an enjoyable experience for me. I avoid seeing movies which contain subject matter filled with horror and excessive violence. The portrayal of the beating that Jesus received at the hands of the Romans sickened me. None of us have suffered such as Jesus, yet He is our example. I do not understand how God the Father could allow His son to suffer so much for us. Nor did Jesus deserve to suffer that kind of ignominious death. The extent of the love of God is beyond my comprehension. Our response to an unjust world and our willingness to suffer for His cause are fundamental to being Christ-like.

LIVING WITH PAIN

I daily live with some of persistent pain. Caring for me is my primary physician, a wonderful person who provides excellent care for me. On a professional level, I also prepare her corporate taxes. The issue of pain management is always a part of our discussions whenever we have an occasion to speak to each other. She once commented that I was the type of person who could loose a finger and then ask for aspirin and a Band-Aid. She has attempted to get me to agree to begin taking an antidepressant, based on the logic that, since one has cancer, they therefore must be depressed. She is also quick to prescribe pain inhibitors. Though quite effective in blocking pain, they take away my ability to think clearly. As a result, I have elected not to use them. My goal is to minimize as much as possible the use of medication. Although society teaches us to avoid pain at all cost, as Christians I believe that we should allow it to bring about change in our lives. Learning to deal with pain affords us an opportunity to draw closer to God, to pray to Him more intently, and to be more Christ-like. Most people spend more time, energy, and money in an attempt to avoid pain than they do in trying to learn how to deal with it. Suffering is a natural part of life in that God permits it as a means of drawing us closer to him. I am convinced that we can learn endurance and, by extension, perseverance. I may hate the process, but I love the final product.

WHO DO YOU BLAME?

The IRS publishes an annual business plan which is a strategic blueprint for collecting income taxes from the industry sector they believe is the most evasive to the tax laws. Expect a discernible increase of IRS auditors if your industry is on their current business plan. Does Satan have a business plan? I am convinced he does and that you, your church, or your family might be part of it. Job was part of his business plan, and we know what happened to him. The point I am trying to make is that we should be clear in our thinking as to the source of our suffering. God allows Satan to do what we invited him to do through the actions of our first parents, Adam and Eve. I have a sense that God cries with us at the same time that Satan rejoices at us in our pain. In *The Passion of the Christ*, Satan was the shadowy figure moving through the crowd rejoicing at the death of Jesus. I am sure he thought that he had won the battle at the cross. This is the mystery of the Gospel message. The workings of God and Satan are still a mystery to us, yet I place blame on the devil, and not God, for my pain and suffering. I desire to follow the example of how Jesus responded to his sufferings.

God created a perfect world. However, all of us must now suffer pain and death because of the sin of Adam and Eve. Yet this is what grounds my faith: That God created both this world and our final home (heaven) as a perfect place. We are simply living between the fall and a time of perfection, often suffering because of the original sin that corrupted the world and released Satan. Does God feel my pain? I believe He does. On many occasions I would lie in bed at night and cry out to God. "When is it enough?" "When have I suffered enough that you will give me relief from this pain?" His answers were always the same. "My grace is sufficient for you, for my power is made perfect in weakness." God is always there, providing for us a place of rest in the mist of our suffering. I have learned much from my suffering: Life is hard, yet God is good. Life is not fair, but God is good.

MY HEROES:

Joseph is one of my great heroes of the Bible. His is a remarkable story of suffering and triumph. He was rejected by his own family and sold as a slave. Falsely accused of adultery and sentenced to jail. He was even betrayed by his friends while imprisoned. Joseph was certainly one who had good reason to be bitter about his life! But his is also a story about the management training program of God. Joseph first learned to run a large family household and then a sizeable government facility (the jail). Finally he was appointed to run an entire nation, one of the largest of its time. God prepared him for each task through great personal suffering. I am certain that Joseph did not appreciate his time in jail, but he could see how God used it for His glory. His heart remained tender through all his trials and he always gave God the credit for his abilities. Joseph believed that God was always in control and that His grace continually flowed down to him. His words to his brothers regarding their selling him into slavery reveal a true perspective on life. *"You intended to harm me, but God intended it for good to accomplish what is now being done, the saving of many lives."* Genesis 50:20. His brothers could not comprehend the bigger picture painted by God and, sometimes, neither do we.

Another of my heroes is Mother Theresa of Calcutta. She once said, "Never let anything so fill you with sorrow as to make you forget the joy of Christ risen.[3] What impresses me most about Mother Theresa? She often said that she would pray "Lord deliver me from _____" (you can fill in the blank). The answer God gave her was always the same, "Mother Theresa, accept it." Yet this is a problem with most of us. We are unwilling to accept our suffering as a means of spiritual transformation. We resist the very purpose for which God allows it to come about.

[3] Women's Devotional Bible Calendar, 12/22 (my birthday).

THREE OPTIONS:

We have basically three options from which to choose:

1. You can blame God.
2. You can be in denial of the problem.
3. You can learn to suffer well.

Our lives will never be completely free of pain and suffering. We can learn to grow spiritually through suffering or blame God for our troubles. It is easy to place the blame on God. We rationalize that, because He is in control, He let it (whatever "it" might be) happen. (There is also the theory known as "open theism" which takes the position that God was just as surprised as the rest of us during Sept. 11th. attack on the World Trade Center.) I often remind myself that humanity opened the door for Satan when Adam and Eve chose to know both good and evil. (Though their actions might have been unintentional, perhaps, I certainly do not pretend to know the mindset of either at the time of the fall.) (Genesis 3:5). It was we humans who changed the equation, not God. It is my belief that He continues to desire that which is best for us here on earth and gives us a promise of it in heaven. Does God allow natural events to take their own course? Most often He does. Does He sometimes answer our prayers for healing? Yes, He does that as well, but the reason why He permits one outcome and not the other is known to Him alone. I know not the reason why I have cancer. It may have been from pesticides in my food or a contaminated water supply. What I do know is that God is using my suffering for His glory.

Denial is a problematic matter. I do not pretend to be any sort of psychologist and so I will leave treatment advice to others better trained in the field of counseling. I know friends who are in denial. They smile on the outside but are crying within. They often have the same dream night after night as their subconscious tries to process the pain. My suggestion is that you seek professional assistance if you are in denial.

NEW EYES:

Living – and suffering – with cancer has given me a new set of eyes with which to see the world. The Apostle Paul spoke of this eloquently in 2 Corinthians 4:18, *"We fix our eyes not on what is seen but what is not seen.* What is seen is temporary, what is unseen is eternal. Facing mortality has made the first death more appealing, as long as it comes quickly. The problem with death is that there is always more than one victim. Loved ones also suffer with loss and must continue on alone after you have passed. As a child I often reflected on the line from the John Donne poem "For Whom the Bell Tolls" which reads, *"Therefore, never send to know / For whom the bell tolls, / It tolls for thee."*[4] The loss of a loved one – for whatever reason – can be the cause of tremendous pain and suffering. There is a blues lyric that says *"that which doesn't kill you makes you stronger."* This is not true from a physical perspective. A person is usually damaged for life if they receive chemotherapy and live to tell about it. But this can be real from a spiritual perspective. You become a better person if you are transformed in your suffering into being more Christ-like.

I have no interest in owning anything having now a clear view of eternity. You can not take it with you when you die. And so, unless your family wants what you have or can sell it, you might as well give it away.

[4] Hemingway, Ernest, For Whom the Bell Tolls, published by Simon and Schuster, New York, New York.

I use to enjoy traversing rivers in my boat. I still do, but not to the extent I once did before becoming terminally ill. I have a new sense of urgency relative to time. I want to spend what remains of my life helping others and making an impact on their lives for Jesus Christ.

You have probably heard this question posed numerous times: "What would you do with your life if you only had two weeks to live?" Most people would respond by announcing that they either would take a trip around the world or intend to spend quality time visiting with their family. Hollywood has produced a plethora of movies dealing with the topic of an individual having a short life expectancy. Most recently was the film *Life or Something Like It,* starring Angelina Jolie. My answer to the aforementioned question, and one I think most Christians would give, is to do what they believe that God has called them to do. God has called me to be a teacher and that will be my passion until He calls me home. True satisfaction comes only from obeying the will of God for your life.

Living with cancer has also given me the opportunity to come to know new souls that I would not have otherwise met. The person who takes samples of my blood is named Pinky. (Her real name is Vanessa.) Every time I visit Pinky she asks me the same question: "You have cancer but does cancer have you?" My initial reaction was to respond "Yes, it does have me. I am in its grip." She would ask the same question during subsequent visits. Pinky is a professing Christian and, after pondering her question for several visits, I started to realize just what she was asking. Cancer does not have me as long as I am a child of the King. Jesus said,

"Therefore I tell you, do not worry about your life, what you will eat or drink; or about your body, what you will wear. Is not life more important than food, and the body more important than clothes?" (Matthew 6:25, NIV). The physical nature is not all there is to life. The first death is separation from the body and the second death is separation from God. I fully expect to experience the first death but not the second. Nothing, not the dark powers of the world or a terminal illness can separate us from the love of God. (Romans 8:38ff).

LET ME SUMMARIZE FOR YOU WHAT I HAVE LEARNED ABOUT SUFFERING:

1. I believe that God allows suffering in our lives to mold and shape us into the image of Jesus Christ.
2. Suffering is not necessarily the result of sin in our lives.
3. People of God people suffer as a part of spiritual transformation.
4. Faith believes that God knows more about life than I do.
5. Who are we to comprehend the vastness of God?
6. One of the hardest parts of complete surrender to the will of God is that we will never know the reason why until we get to heaven.
7. A strange sense of the presence of God comes over you (giving you a feeling of never being alone) when people pray for you.
8. We do not know the timing of God.

9. We were born to die. God is patiently waiting for us to get to heaven, perhaps to start our true calling.

10. I believe that the key to suffering well is preparation and that each one of us should work on building our capacity to suffer.

11. Life wears us down, but it can also make us malleable and useful for His good purpose.

12. God is always there to rebuild our lives through the work of the Holy Spirit.

13. Life is full of so many more possibilities if you open yourself to the providence of God.

14. How we respond to an unjust world and how much we are willing to suffer for the cause of Christ is of primary importance to being Christ-like.

15. I am convinced that we can learn endurance and perseverance through suffering. I might find the process distasteful, but I love the final product.

16. I blame the devil – and not God – for my pain and suffering. I look at how Jesus responded to His sufferings as my example.

17. You have three options as to how one can respond to suffering: You can blame God. You can live in denial of the problem. Or you can learn to suffer well.

18. True satisfaction comes from obeying the will of God for your life no matter how long you have to live.

Discussion Questions for

Accounting
THROUGH
THE EYES OF
FAITH

One Question per Chapter,
in sequence except 13,
Devotions in Accounting:

A bachelors or masters degree in business at many academic institutions would not contain a strong liberal arts component. Why do many of the Christian Colleges such as Eastern University design the business curriculum to include courses on justice and cross-cultural issues? Would this time be better utilized in "pure" business topics like accounting or finance?

It is clear that the financial community and governmental agencies are demanding more from accountants: more honesty, a greater understanding of business processes and increased fraud detection procedures. The scandals has also created an unusual public reaction, it has smashed the old perception of accounting as being dull and boring. Suddenly accountants are called upon to be detectives and forensic investigators ready to provide insight into fraudulent financial activity and wrongdoing. Accounting has always attracted "numbers people." Does the accounting profession now demand a new type of personality to meet the challenge of rooting out fraud? What do you think would be the perfect qualities of a successful modern day Certified Public Accountant?

Explain the spiritual linkage between Leviticus 25 and Luke 4:21. How is Jesus the personification of the year of Jubilee? Using your knowledge of accounting and finance, why is sin described as a liability account and salvation as the cancellation of debt?

What is the linkage between accounting and justice? Why was the church so concerned about the development of a comprehensive accounting system when economic commerce began to flourish internationally?

International trade can often improve the economic condition of a country and its people. The raising of debt and equity for business ventures in less developed nations is difficult to impossible without an extensive knowledge of financial markets and international accounting standards. Technology is making the task easier, but international accounting standards struggle to find acceptance. How would one universally accepted accounting standard improve the raising of debt and equity for small business ventures around the world?

You are a U.S. citizen and you work for World Vision International in Monrovia CA. You have been out of the U.S. for 350 days during the last tax year. A friend has mentioned that you might not be subject to U.S. income tax because of the length of time you have been away from the U.S. You want to resolve this important tax issue. How would you **begin your research** assuming you do not have access to a U.S. Internal Revenue Office (IRS) or other professional tax preparer? (You are not required to find the correct number of days.)

You are considering doing relief work in a country not currently served by any major relief organizations. You want to create a feeder organization in the United States for the purpose of raising funds for this new relief effort. What are the major financial criteria for public charity status in the United States?

What is the role of the Certified Public Accountant as auditor and/or consultant in the environmental debate? What are the critical environmental issues for auditors? What is the first step in the audit planning process from an environmental perspective?

If you were given a choice between living in a socialist society, a communist society, a capitalist society or under a benevolent dictatorship, in total support of the freedom of religion where 90% of the citizens were Christian believers; which would you choose? Do you agree or disagree that Christianity teaches and supports the principles of liberty?

Our very existence depends on the physical provisions of food, clothing and shelter. We don't want these necessities of life to be temporary. In fact, we want them to be as permanent and stable as possible. So why does Jesus teach us to pray every day for our daily bread? How truly trustworthy is material wealth in our modern society considering the destructive force of hurricanes like Katrina?

The Bible teaches us that the Earth and everything in it belongs to God, including each one of us. It is a hard concept to comprehend. We are in fact more managers than owners of the things we consider our own. Does our style and mode of stewardship, the allocation of time, talent, natural resources and money, flow from our understanding of this difficult concept? What is the basis of how you make the decision to give God your money, time and talent?

Christian friend has just learned that you are enrolled in a business program. They come to you and express their concern that you will be seduced by worldly pleasures and concerns. They wonder how a true Christian can be a good business student or businessperson. How would you explain to your friend your academic interest in pursuing a business degree? What does it mean to be called to a Godly standard in business?

What would you do with your life if you were told that you only had two weeks to live? What about two years? What about six years?

To order copies of the book

Accounting

Through the Eyes of Faith

$29.97 + 2.50 (S&H)

online at:
http://www.BooksToBelieveIn.com/Textbooks.php

by phone:
have your credit card handy and call:
(303) 794-8888

by fax:
(720) 863-2013

by mail: send check payable to:
Thornton Publishing, Inc.
17011 Lincoln Ave. #408
Parker, Colorado 80134

If it is temporarily sold out at your favorite bookstore,
have them order more of **ISBN: 0-9779960-6-9**

Name: _____

Address: _____

_____

Phone: _____

E-mail: _____

Credit Card #: _____

Card Type: _____ Expiration Date: _____/ _____

Security Code: _____

CONTENTS

Table of Contents

PART IV – Accounting and Moral Philosophy

DISCLAIMER

Accounting Through the Eyes of Faith is an anthology of chapters written by Christian accountants, finance professionals or theologians and compiled by Dr. Jack E. Bower of Eastern University. This book was **not done** in collaboration or sponsorship with the Council of Christian Colleges & Universities; nor did it receive assistance in any manner or form from the Council of Christian Colleges & Universities, which discontinued a series of books with a similar title and theme published by Harper Collins Publishers.

ADVISORY BOARD

The Eastern University accounting faculty served as the Advisory Board for compiling the third edition. Members of the Advisory Board are as follows:

> Jack E. Bower, CPA, Chair
> Mary Jo Jones, CPA
> Robin Lowery, CPA

Those wishing to submit chapters for the fourth edition should contact Professor Bower for details. Chapters do not necessarily represent the views of the complier, the advisory board, or Eastern University. Responsibility for opinions expressed and accuracy of facts rests solely with the author(s) of each chapter.